HAUNTED
DURHAM

HAUNTED
DURHAM

Darren W. Ritson

> *To my wonderful partner Jayne Watson*
> *and our beautiful daughter Abbey May Ritson*

Frontispiece: The famous towers of Durham Cathedral as seen from the River Wear.

First published 2010

The History Press
The Mill, Brimscombe Port
Stroud, Gloucestershire, GL5 2QG
www.thehistorypress.co.uk

ISBN 978 0 7524 5410 8

Typesetting and origination by The History Press
Printed in Great Britain

CONTENTS

ACKNOWLEDGEMENTS

Particular thanks to Mike Hallowell for supplying me with some great ghost tales regarding the historic city that is Durham. Massive thanks must also go to Julie Olley for the artist's impressions and illustrations that are featured herein. To Drew Bartley, Fiona Vipond, Lee Stephenson, Mark Winter, Paul Dixon and Ralph Keeton (my fellow GHOST members). To Karen Hague, Adam Hague and Meg Armstrong from Witton Castle who provided me with information regarding the castle's history, its ghost stories and of course allowing overnight access to investigate, also thanks to Andrew Local for negotiating the investigation with the owners of the castle and for the use of his pictures of the castle and grounds. To Paul Mash and his family from the Garden House Hotel, Paul Wray from the City Hotel, the owners and staff from the old church hall, and Margaret Wilkinson and Dave Williams from the Dog and Gun pub. To Mike and Audrey Leonard of the Dun Cow pub on Old Elvet, and Paddy and Irene from the Shakespeare Tavern on Saddler Street. To Keith and Maggie Bell for all their help and assistance in regards to the history and ghosts of Crook Hall and for their friendly welcome into their wonderful home. To Paul and Diane Martin from the Fighting Cocks, and of course to my anonymous informant, the bar supervisor. Thanks also go to my good friends Cindy and Colin Nunn for the use of pictures and information in regards to Vane Tempest Hall. My gratitude must also go to the Newcastle Libraries and Information Service – particularly Sarah Mulligan, for assisting and supplying me with the wonderful old images of Durham. Sincere thanks must go to all those who have contributed in some way to my research and with the compilation of this book. Finally, my thanks go to the staff at The History Press, especially Beth Amphlett for having faith in me. All photographs in the book were taken by Darren W. Ritson unless otherwise stated.

Other books by Darren W. Ritson and published by The History Press include: *The South Shields Poltergeist: One Family's Fight Against an Invisible Intruder* (with Michael J. Hallowell), and *Haunted Newcastle*. In preparation and coming soon – *Haunted Berwick* and *Ghosts at Christmas*.

INTRODUCTION

The City of Durham is a place of aesthetic beauty, charm and character and is one of my favourite places in the North of England. Immortalised by Roger Whittaker in his 1969 top twenty hit *Durham Town (The Leavin')*, Durham City is a condensed metropolis that offers a wide range of amenities. There is plenty for the visitor to see and do in Durham City and quite often, when I venture down its little old side streets and crooked cobbled lanes, soaking up the ambience and its historic environs, it takes my breath away. Like Newcastle-upon-Tyne (and many other historic townships), Durham is awash with reminders of the past and wherever you go, and whatever you do, you are never far from something that has a historical connection and may be of interest.

The City of Durham.

If you were to just stop for a minute, and take time out from a busy schedule to observe your surroundings – and this relates to almost everywhere – you would be astounded to spot things you probably never noticed before. Architecture, structural designs, pillars, posts, old engravings on the ancient buildings that give clues as to what they were in times gone by – you'd really be amazed!

The City of Durham is located about 17 miles south of Newcastle-upon-Tyne and 11 miles south-west of Sunderland and is commonly associated with its student population, its magnificent constructions and architecture, the Northumbrian saint who goes by the name of Cuthbert, and is recognised across the world as being the true home to English mustard. It has a meandering river with tight bends that creates the peninsula which central Durham sits upon. The cathedral, Durham Castle, Palace Green and the university are all nestled upon this wonderful isthmus and, given its great height, these edifices tower above the rest of the city and thus dominate the surrounding areas. At the foot of the peninsula stands the historic market square or market place, where of course regular markets and bazaars still take place. Close by there is also the indoor market which provides shelter and protection from the elements for the busy city centre shoppers.

Durham takes its name from the old words 'Dun' which means hill and 'Holm' which comes from Old Norse and means island – Dun Holm. Over the years it has had a number of epithets ranging from the Nordic Dun Holm, and Duresme after the Normans renamed it during their

Durham market place in 1850. (Courtesy of Newcastle Libraries and Information Service)

Durham Cathedral and Castle seen from afar and towering over the city's rooftops.

occupation of the area, to Dunelm, as it was known in Latin. Nowadays, of course, we all know the city as Durham, but according to the celebrated historian Robert Surtees (1779-1834) in his *History and Antiquities of the County Palatine of Durham* (1816), he states that, 'it is an impossibility to tell when the city's modern name came into being.'

Archaeological evidence suggests that people have been residing in this area for over 2,000 years with the origins of the city's name (argued by some) tracing back to when a group of monks from Lindisfarne settled there with the remains of St Cuthbert. This dates back to around AD 995. It is said that these travelling monks, who had just ended a three-day fast during their journey, came across a young milkmaid near Mount Joy. The milkmaid declared to the monks that she was looking for her 'Dun Cow', which according to the milkmaid had been seen last in what is now Durham City. The monks considered this 'divine intervention', and so followed the milkmaid to a steep wooded hill that was surrounded by the River Wear. It was there that they settled and began laying the foundations for a great cathedral. The twelfth-century chronicler and a monk of Durham Priory, known as the Symeon of Durham, believed that this cathedral was the very first building in the City of Durham. The first street in Durham is said to be called 'Dun Cow Lane', which stands directly to the east of the great cathedral itself.

'All very intriguing information,' I hear you say, 'but where are the ghosts?'

Well, Durham, like everywhere else, has its fair share of folklore and ghost tales, with a lot of these tales of the supernatural surviving through the years to this day. In fact, the legend of the aforementioned 'Dun Cow' itself originates from the tale that brings us the suspected origin of the city's name. The Dun Cow was allegedly a mystical beast that belonged to a giant who was slain by Guy of Warwick. The animal was subsequently allowed to live and feed in an area known as Mitchell's Fold, which is a Bronze Age stone circle in the Shropshire area where, legend has it, King Arthur pulled the sword from the stone. The traditional folk story suggests that this cow could produce an endless supply of milk at any given time, so when a local woman filled her bucket and then became greedy and tried to fill another (some say a local witch used her powers and milked it dry), the cow left the area and found its way to Warwickshire. As punishment, the witch was then turned to stone and surrounded by other stones in an effort to confuse her and stop her from escaping. The penalty evidently worked, if you believe in folklore, as the witch's stone is still there for all to see today.

As with most folktales and legends there are numerous versions of the story, with the above being the most favoured. Some say it was the actual cow that was slain by Guy of Warwick and not the giant, but if this was the case it makes me wonder how the cow came to be lost by the milkmaid near Durham — after all, according to this version it had been slain. My guess (to put together a sensible workable scenario) is that it was the giant who was slain and the cow somehow found its way up North where it was subsequently looked after (and then lost) by the milkmaid.

There are many other stories of ghosts, wraiths, and spectral visitors that are associated with Durham. Some are the more well-known ghost tales that the city has, however, others are not so well-known stories that I have managed to uncover with the help of a good friend of mine, Mike — who also researches the paranormal — and it is largely down to these stories that this volume was cobbled together. Certain narratives contained herein were discovered from old

A magnificent sculptured statue of six monks depicting the bringing of St Cuthbert's remains to Durham — his final resting place.

newspaper cuttings that had been archived away in a private collection for a long time. In my book *In Search of Ghosts* (2008) Mike Hallowell graciously penned the afterword, and in it he sums up why he feels it is important to rescue these old cases:

Years ago I inherited a fading, yellowed newspaper cutting from a good friend. It was dated 1923, and told the story of a Scottish crofter's house that was haunted by the spirit of an old shepherd. The cutting was incredibly brief, and simply mentioned the name of the village, the name of the crofter and the appearance of the old man in his living room. Pretty much par for the course in ghost-hunting circles, of course, but there was something about this particular tale that intrigued me. I began to dig, and uncovered a wealth of information that allowed me to breathe fresh life into the story and write it up as a newspaper feature. The life of a story is in the detail, for it allows the reader to visualise what occurred much more accurately. It also sets the context and can reanimate a dried-out old legend for the benefit of a whole new generation, which may never have heard it before.

'To breathe fresh life into the story.' In fact, the idea of reviving these old tales, preventing them from being lost in the sands of time, is a concept that Mike Hallowell adheres to and has done for years, firmly believing (with good reason) that had these stories not been salvaged and re-researched, they would have been lost forever, and how sad would that have been?

Over the years Mike has resurrected and re-told literally hundreds of ghost legends and folkloric tales in his newspaper column and for this we must thank him. Being motivated by the way Mike works has enabled me to do similar things with some of my book projects, with many of these old ghost stories being featured in both *Haunted Newcastle* (2009) and of course this volume *Haunted Durham*.

So, before you get relaxed in your favourite armchair, be sure to pour yourself a drink, dim those lights, settle down comfortably and prepare yourself for a profusion of paranormal peculiarities that are truly blood-curdling to the core. Oh…and don't think for one minute that there are any untruths weaved into these eerie narratives, on the contrary, to the best of my knowledge they are all true.

The old cobbled road known as Dun Cow Lane, believed to be the very first road in Durham City.

one

THE GHOSTS OF DURHAM

Durham Castle

Where better to begin a tour of haunted Durham than at this magnificent Norman castle. There can be very few castles in England as perfectly placed as the castle at Durham City, and less still, so wonderfully neighboured. Durham Castle and its Palace Green counterpart (the cathedral) occupy the area on top of the embankment that is flanked with stunning woodland and aesthetic beauty, and is almost completely looped by the winding River Wear. Because of its superb position, the castle was able to withstand many a battle and siege, including two

Durham Castle viewed from Framwellgate Bridge, c. 1900. (Courtesy of Newcastle Libraries and Information Service)

famous invasions from the Scottish kings Duncan and Malcolm III. Their efforts at taking Durham Castle were, like most others, total failures.

The castle was built by order of King William a few years after the Norman Conquest of 1066 and is a magnificent example of the early motte-and-bailey construction that was so favoured by the Normans. Appointed by the king, the Bishop of Durham was given royal authority on his behalf and subsequently the castle became the Bishop's seat. It remained the Bishop's seat (known as the Bishop's Palace) until they found a more suitable venue in nearby Bishop Auckland. Then, what was once their primary residence and castle, was converted into a college. This was around 1840.

The college/university is one of the most impressive universities in the UK with a giant Great Hall that was created by Antony Bek – the Prince Bishop of Durham – in the early fourteenth century. Known as the longest Great Hall in Britain until the fifteenth century (until it was shortened by Bishop Richard Foxe – 1448-1528), this magnificent structure is adorned with much military memorabilia including artefacts and *objets d'art* from the Civil War and the Napoleonic Wars. Portraits of the past bishops and university dons decorate the spectacularly high walls with the lower half of them being covered in a beautiful oak wood panelling.

Situated between the Great Hall and Bishop Pudsey's Building is the Black Staircase. The Black Staircase is named after the dark oak wood that was used to make it in around 1662, and reaches almost 6oft in height. The staircase was at first a free-standing structure using nothing but the walls for its support, but nowadays there are smooth and circular columns that keep

A gardener tends to his lawn in this 1920s picture of the courtyard in Durham Castle. Now used by students. (Courtesy of Newcastle Libraries and Information Service)

it in place. This is where the ghost is said to walk. She is known as the Grey Lady of Durham Castle and is thought to have been the wife of one of the former bishops back in the sixteenth century. Allegedly, this sad and lonely spectre was said to have been depressed when she was alive, so committed suicide by throwing herself over the stairwell banister, falling almost 60ft through the narrow gap between the stairs to her tragic death.

Cleaners and visitors to the castle have seen the ghost many times on the stairwell with most of the sightings occurring at night. Sometimes, it is said, her presence is felt without her spectre actually being seen. In 1987 a local ghost hunter called Brian Smith arranged to spend a night on the castle stairwell in the hope of catching a glimpse of the infamous ghost, but the all-night sit-in was cancelled due to resident students who may have drummed up false phenomena as a joke during his investigation.

To my knowledge, due to this most important detail, the vigil was postponed the first time around and was subsequently rescheduled for later in the year when the students were 'not in residence'. At present, I am unaware if Brian's vigil did take place and efforts to find out have proved fruitless. It would be interesting to know if he managed to carry out this investigation, and more interesting still to find out if he actually caught a glimpse of the phantom. If Brian, or perhaps someone who knows him, is reading this book, then perhaps they will contact him and ask him to get in touch with me to let me know how he got on.

The Grey Lady is not the only spectral visitor linked to the castle. It is thought that the ghost of a university professor hurled himself down another flight of steps at the castle and is reputed

A picture from 1920 of the beautifully ornate and decorated stairwell known as the Black Staircase. Named after the dark oak wood that was used to make it in around 1662, this stairwell is the haunt of Durham Castle's most infamous spectre. (Courtesy of Newcastle Libraries and Information Service)

Owengate, the small cobbled road leading down from the university that is said to be haunted by a former college professor who committed suicide by hurling himself down a flight of stairs.

to haunt the nearby area that is known as Owengate. I don't know what it is with people throwing themselves down flights of stairs to kill themselves at this castle, but it seems that the ghosts that reside there both chose this method to end their lives.

Whatever goes on at the castle in regards to its former visitors, their eerie presences have most certainly been felt, leaving me in no doubt that Durham Castle is one of the most fascinating, and best known locales associated with the ghost lore of Durham City.

The Outraged Wraith

Sometime in the late nineteenth century, in the area where the old rectory in Durham stands, a terrifying paranormal incident allegedly took place that sent shockwaves through all of the local people who heard about it.

A postman on his daily rounds is said to have seen what he described as a 'hooded phantom of a young lad' as he sauntered by the nearby cemetery. After stopping and staring at it for a while he suddenly became aware of 'it' becoming aware of him. At this point he lost his self control and went into a great panic. As fear overcame him, he dropped his bag and ran away petrified.

If you think this was a harrowing experience you will be shocked to learn that the story doesn't end there. Much to the postman's horror, he realised that the spectral boy was in hot pursuit of him and was catching up fast. Upon reaching his home he tore through the house in

An artist's impression of the 'hooded phantom' as seen by the postman as he stands amongst the tombstones. (Illustration by Julie Olley)

A path makes its way through St Margaret's graveyard. This is where the author believes the 'outraged wraith' made his appearance.

a terrible state and ultimately locked himself (and his wife) in a room and barricaded the door in an effort to escape the fury of the irritated phantom.

It is said that the spectre could be heard tearing the room apart next door as the couple trembled with fear. Bangs and crashes were heard as the ghost smashed up the room in sheer anger. After a while the smashing ceased, though it is thought that the postman and his wife didn't come out from the hideaway until at least two hours later. When they did come out they packed their bags and fled the area. Once the locals heard about the postman's encounter, no one dared pass the area of the cemetery – day or night – for fear of the same thing occurring to them. Eventually a local wise woman was called in to sort out the problem and, by all accounts, persuaded the ghost to return to his resting place.

Details of this truly horrifying episode are rather scant to say the least and one wonders why the phantom was so enraged. Perhaps he was annoyed at the postman because he was actually alive and the ghost wasn't? Maybe the spirit of the boy was finding it hard being dead and took his frustrations out on the first person he came across. I get the feeling that the postman was not singled out and targeted by the restless wraith, but was simply in the wrong place at the wrong time. Nevertheless, if the story is true, it does illustrate just how frightening these paranormal occurrences can be.

Old Durham Jail

Durham Jail was built in 1810 to replace an earlier prison and over the years a total of ninety-one people were hanged there. £2,000 cash for the construction of the reformatory was assured by

Durham Jail, built in 1810, houses a former cell (now a storeroom) which is said to be haunted by two spectral inmates who were allegedly seen fighting.

the Bishop of Durham, Shute Barrington (1734-1826) and by 31 July 1809 the building work had begun. Sir Henry Vane Tempest laid the foundation stone and the prison was eventually finished by the English architect and surveyor, Ignatius Bonomi (1787-1870). By 1819 the prison had over 600 holding cells and had taken its first consignment of inmates.

The cells at the old Durham Jail were the one-time holding place for the notorious killer, Mary Ann Cotton. She was one of the felons hanged at Durham Jail in 1873 for the murder of her stepson, Charlie, although she protested her innocence until the last. Nevertheless she was accused of other murders due to the fact that the poison, arsenic, was found in the stomach of her stepson during his autopsy. This discovery led to one of the biggest murder trials in the history of North-East England. It is believed that over twenty people close to her during her twenty-year killing spree died. It has been argued that not all died at her hands, but a large proportion certainly did.

It is not surprising that Durham Jail has a ghost or two. With so much negative energy bounding around the place after years of misery and death, it doesn't come as much of a revelation that a room on the ground floor was abandoned as a 'cell' and turned into a store room because of the two ghosts that allegedly haunted it. In the winter of 1947 two prisoners became engaged in a skirmish that resulted in one of the inmates stabbing the other to death with a kitchen knife. After having had prior disagreements with his cell mate, the prisoner had somehow managed to smuggle in the blade, following kitchen duties, with the sole intention of stabbing him if more arguments developed. Arguments did ensue and thus the brutal murder took place.

The prisoner was relocated to a new cell following the murder, with the cell where the actual murder took place being reused for new prisoners – but not for long. After being left in the murder cell overnight, the wardens found a prisoner cowering in the corner shaking in absolute terror. Ashen-faced and trembling, the inmate told the wardens that he had seen (what was to be coined after the event) the 're-enactment' of the murder in ghostly form. He went on to say that the murder had replayed itself silently in front of him until the two figures faded away into thin air. Word began to circulate around the prison resulting in the other prisoners flatly refusing to occupy that particular prison cell. After a while the wardens closed down the cell and converted it into a store room for linen and other such effects. To my knowledge, the ghosts have never been seen since.

The Grey Tower

Not far from Framwellgate Bridge lies North Road. Walking along North Road is, in all honesty, a rather pleasant experience. North Road is adorned with many old and wonderful buildings; well, the section of the road that joins on from 'Crossgate' is. Once you actually head under the railway bridge and venture up the section of North Road that leads you to the A691 (Framwellgate Peth), you are greeted with a long stretch of thoroughfare that is lined with tall trees and woodland. There are a number of buildings on this stretch of road tucked away behind the dense foliage, but one of the most striking places of interest is an old construction known as the Grey Tower which overlooks North Road near to where St Leonard's School stands.

The Grey Tower on North Road is thought to date from the late eighteenth century and is reputedly haunted by a lady who has been seen gazing out from one of the windows.

An artist's impression of the 'ghost lady' who has been seen in the Grey Tower window. (Illustration by Julie Olley)

The Grey Tower is a magnificent privately-owned building that is thought to date from the late eighteenth century, but there is a possibility that its foundations may be several centuries older; the tower certainly takes on a medieval look, with its battlements high upon the roof and its impressive, and very grand, stone walls.

The tower, many years ago, belonged to a well-known journalist from Durham called Frank Rushford who for many years of his life – almost twenty I believe – edited the *Durham Advertiser*. It was Rushford himself who labelled the Grey Tower 'the haunted house' due to a ghostly tale that was allegedly connected to the place. To understand the origins of the ghost story, however, we need to delve a little further back into the house's history. To do this I contacted Mike Hallowell, who is a bit of an authority on the folklore and ghost legends of North-East England. I thought if anyone knew the history of the Grey Tower, he would. I wasn't wrong.

After contacting Mike and enquiring about the case, I was invited to delve into his rather enormous collection of ghost stories, literature and archives that are neatly and meticulously packed away in his office under the stairs. It didn't take us long to dig up the information I was looking for as we soon discovered an old newspaper clipping from many years ago which, unfortunately, was not dated. We also discovered a piece of writing that Mike had prepared that summarised the tower's history and ghost legends, and so I felt it was my duty to reprint it within these pages, verbatim – of course with Mike's full consent.

Back in the 1860s, the Grey Tower was the home of the Victorian novelist Isabella Varley, otherwise known as Mrs Linnaeus Banks and Isabella Varley-Banks. Varley specialised in writing gothic horror novels, and the Grey Tower gained some notoriety when it was the setting of the story *The Waif of Wearside*. She also made it the setting of her tale *Stung to the Quick*. It was around this time, it seems, that the tale of the tower being haunted started to circulate. The Grey Tower was no stranger to speculation. Locals believed – probably correctly – that a long tunnel led from the tower to Finchale Priory, and local children would often run past the place instead of walking due to the alleged presence of the ghost.

But just who was it that was supposed to haunt the tower? No one really knows, but numerous witnesses claimed to have seen the pallid, ghostly face of a woman staring down at them from the window of one of the upper rooms. Reports of the 'Lady of the Grey Tower' date back at least to the 1880s.

Dressed in a grey smock, she would gaze down mournfully as if reminiscing over some sad event. Chillingly, the event may well have been a murder. Details are sketchy, but it seems that a young woman may have been cruelly robbed of her life on the doorstep of the main entrance. Local legend has it that the doorstep forever remained wet after the murder, even in the best of weather.

Although this story is probably an old wives' tale, at least one former resident admitted that, after scrubbing the step, it seemed to stay wet for an inordinate length of time. Isabella Varley was seen in the literary world as the successor of Ann Radcliffe, who in the summer of 1794 had published a horror novel entitled *The Mysteries of Udolpho*. The tale follows the adventures of Emily St Aubert who – and here's the clue – is forced to endure supernatural torments in an eerie old castle. Varley admitted that her 'chief inducement to come to the tower was because of its uncanny reputation as a haunted dwelling.'

Like Frank Rushford, Varley's husband George was a newspaper editor. George died of cancer in 1882, and Isabella passed away in 1897. By this time, though, they had long since departed from the Grey Tower. The Grey Tower has had a long and intriguing history so who knows what spectres still watch over it, fondly – or sadly – remembering days gone by.

The South Street Coach

Near New Elvet stands the County Hotel, on the spot where Lady M. Radcliffe, the sister of James Radcliffe (or Radclyffe), the 3rd Earl of Derwentwater, once lived. The 3rd Earl of Derwentwater's family seat was, of course, Dilston Castle in Northumberland.

The Jacobite rising of 1715 against George I had failed, and during an abundance of arrests made thereafter, James Radcliffe was beheaded at the Tower of London. Due to the powers that be, the authorities decided to let his decapitated corpse be transported back to his homeland. His head, as it happens, was also retained and brought back to the North where, apparently, it was sewn back on before his body was given a decent burial. After his burial at his family seat in Northumberland, the folk of old Durham town began to see the headless spectre of the Earl as he thundered down South Street on his phantom coach.

Many people are said to have witnessed this spectral vision, terrifying them as you can imagine, yet some Durham folk were left bewildered as to why the spectral coach should rattle its way down South Street. South Street is actually across the River Wear from Elvet so there is no know reason, to my knowledge, as to why the ghost is seen there.

Dilston Castle in Northumberland was the seat of the 3rd Earl of Derwentwater, who is now said to be the ghost that haunts South Street in Durham. For whatever reason, his ghoulish apparition has been seen thundering down South Street on a phantom coach with horses.

South Street, where the spectral coach, horses, and Earl have been seen.

'Why didn't the Earl choose to haunt Dilston Castle where he lived?' I hear you all ask. Well, to be honest, he is reported to. It is not unknown for ghosts to haunt more than one location, with such personages as Anne Boleyn, Mary Queen of Scots and King Henry VIII being good examples. They all haunt an abundance of historic locales and all of these hauntings are very well documented. James Radcliffe seems to be no different, with his spectre – some people say – being seen as it looks down from one of the windows at Dilston Castle. Rumours also persist to this day that he and his soldiers can be heard galloping near the castle as they head off to war.

The Earl hasn't been witnessed for many years now, at Dilston or in Durham's South Street and one wonders why. Has he given up his haunting? Perhaps after all these years he has managed to find rest. Whatever has happened to the Earl of Derwentwater, he can bask in the knowledge that he left behind one of the most terrifying spectres to haunt Durham's streets.

Fred, the Café Ghost

'Ghost stalks the café' was the headline in one of the North-East's most read newspapers back in February 1979 after reports of 'strange goings on' were allegedly witnessed by visitors and staff alike back in the late 1970s. 'Spooked by a ghostly customer' at what was once one of Durham City's most popular shops and cafeterias, led some staff to literally dread going into work. (I think most people still dread going to work, even when there isn't a potentially scary haunting taking place.) One member of staff almost resigned from her employment at the café after the spook made itself known to her.

One day, when she was setting up shop, it is said that she heard a disembodied voice. We know it was disembodied as reports tell us that she was in the premises alone and knows for certain that it could not have been any other staff member. When asked to describe what this voice said, reports say that the lady in question didn't know. Apparently, when the voice was heard, it spoke in an indecipherable way – a 'mutter' or a 'murmuring'. This is quite a common facet in haunted properties, as all good ghost hunters should well know. There have been many documented cases where voices have been heard but not understood. Whispering, muttering, murmuring voices are very common indeed so it comes as no surprise that the woman could not make out what was being said. Mind you, there are of course many cases where disembodied voices are understood and are perfectly decipherable.

Nonetheless, this muttering voice that was heard in the café was enough to scare the witness to the point of sheer terror. The phantom also made its presence known to others. On one occasion it is said to have left not one, but two ladies who were visiting the café white with fright, after they had come in for afternoon tea. Details, I am afraid, are scant as to what happened that day and much digging and subsequent research have not provided me with the answers. What I do know is that the girls never returned to that café again. Something obviously scared them and I would love to know what it was. Perhaps the two ladies in question are reading these very words now, remembering exactly what happened that day. If it was indeed you, please drop me a line and let me know what happened.

The 'shop' area of the premises was affected by the haunting too. The section that sold books was often found to be all 'messed up with the new books' in the morning when staff turned up for work. Many a time, staff would find these 'new books' displaced, either on the floor, or on other shelves where they were not previously left – perhaps they had a phantom librarian – or some entity that was obsessed with sorting or moving the new books, leaving the old ones where they stood?

After a while, the haunting became 'an everyday thing' to the point where the staff who worked at the shop gave the ghost a name, 'Fred'. Fred made his presence felt on many other occasions during his visits to the shop with another particularly frightening encounter being witnessed by yet another two girls. On this occasion they were standing next to the great big stove in the café area near to the kitchens when suddenly the whole room went ice-cold. Then, from directly behind the two girls, came a guttural breath or sigh. When they turned around they found no one standing behind them. They were frightened for many hours after the event. Even the (then) manageress, Mrs Cathy Barras, said 'I must admit I do not like being in the building alone and I make sure I am never the first person in in the mornings – after all, the building dates back to the sixteenth century and must be steeped in history.'

1979 was a long time ago and one wonders what became of the ghost. In fact, during the research for this book, and on one of my many trips to Durham, I attempted to locate the premises and make an effort to speak to the people who reside there now, to see if the phantom still makes his presence known. All I had was a photograph that was given to me by Mike Hallowell, which in turn was given to him by fellow researcher, Alan Tedder, and the newspaper article that went to print in 1979. Using this information, I successfully managed to locate the area in question only to be told, 'there are no ghosts in here young man.'

Silver Street leading up to the market square in central Durham in the early 1900s. 'Fred,' the café ghost, allegedly haunted a shop in this area back in 1979. (Courtesy of Newcastle Libraries and Information Service)

The fact remains though that at one time, in days gone by, a ghost or haunting of some sort did indeed take place in a one-time café/shop in Durham City and had it not been for Alan Tedder, Mike Hallowell, and of course your present author, the story of Fred the café ghost may have been lost into the sands of time, never to be read about and heard of again. At least now the story is back in black and white and has been preserved within these pages for future generations to read, and hopefully, enjoy.

The Haunted Coffee Shop on Elvet Bridge

Elvet Bridge was built by Hugh Puiset (or Pudsey), the Bishop of Durham (1153-1195) as a second bridge to the city. Out of the fourteen arches that were made, only ten are visible as they span the River Wear linking the Elvet area to Central Durham. Under the bridge at the west end we have a former house of correction that is now a pub called Jimmy Allen's, which we will visit later on in this book when we look at the haunted pubs of Durham. It is, however, the premises above Jimmy Allen's bar that we take a brief look at now.

Back in the 1990s it was reported that a one-time coffee shop was subject to some 'ghostly goings on' when, for no reason, the grandfather clock that had never undergone any problems

A view of Elvet Bridge and old Durham City from the late 1800s. (Courtesy of Newcastle Libraries and Information Service)

An artist's impression of the 'phantom lady' seen stoking the fire in the former coffee shop above Jimmy Allen's on Elvet Bridge. (Illustration by Julie Olley)

A more modern view of Elvet Bridge and Durham City, 2009.

since it was made, suddenly stopped and refused to work. Nothing peculiar there, perhaps it just came to the end of its long life? The odd thing, however, is that the clock only stopped working after a number of sightings of an apparition. The ghost seen was that of a woman bending over and stoking a fire. No one knows who she was, or why she began to appear. The thought occurs that she may have something to do with the grandfather clock in some way, but without more information and witness testimony I guess we will never know for sure.

The White Lady of Crook Hall

Crook Hall is located north of Durham City – about five minutes' walk from the Gala Theatre – and stands in majestic surroundings close to the Radisson Hotel. The thirteenth-century hall provides a dramatic background to its stunning gardens and is a place of serenity and extreme beauty. People have come from far and wide to share in the eternal magic of Crook Hall and depart inspired by these heavenly English gardens.

The original Crook Hall was built on lands that belonged to Sidgate Manor and was named after Peter del Croke, who possessed the home in the early fourteenth century. Incidentally, the Manor of Sidgate was granted to Aimeric, the nephew of the Archdeacon Aimeric. His descendants, including the famous American writer, Ralph Waldo Emerson, have been traced to the present day.

The enchanting and wonderfully haunted Crook Hall. The author spent a very interesting afternoon there during his research and was welcomed warmly by his hosts, Keith and Maggie Bell.

Crook Hall is now the family home to Keith and Maggie Bell and they have always believed that the house and gardens should be open to the public so everyone can experience its natural charm and grandeur. The building is like none other I have seen in the respect that it has three sections that all date from different time periods. Different parts of the house then date from between the early 1200s to 1750. The Grade I listed Medieval Hall is the first building you come to as you make your way up the gentle incline from the entrance gate near to Frankland Lane. The Medieval Hall was built around 1208 although the solar wing, by all accounts, has long disappeared. The hall, with its tall walls of stone and high roof provides the hall with a magnificent taste of medieval life.

Next we have the Jacobean manor house, which was built in 1671. Complete with a circular turret, this section of the hall really does take the visitor back in time. I recall my visit there in May 2009 and was astonished to find myself being taken back to times of long ago. The tranquil surroundings and olde world furniture, combined with the smell of the crackling wood on the open fire really did make this trip a memorable one. The Devil, they say, is in the detail, and it's little observations like this that really grab my attention. All that was needed now was the infamous White Lady to make her appearance, but more of her later.

Finally, there is the Georgian House. Towering three storeys high and festooned with beautiful climbing ivy, this section of the house was built by Henry Hopper (of the Hopper family of Shincliffe) when they purchased the property in 1736. Interestingly, there is an area of land to the north of Crook Hall that is still known as Hopper's Wood. Another point of interest is that Canon James Raine (1791-1858), the antiquary who, among others, caused considerable controversy by opening St Cuthbert's tomb, lived there. During his time at Crook Hall he was visited by the poets William Wordsworth (1770-1850) and John Ruskin (1819-1900).

The house is accompanied by five acres of land with an abundance of beautifully cultivated themed gardens such as the Shakespeare Garden, which is full of plants that would have been around in the days of the great man himself. Other gardens include the Secret Garden, the Georgian Walled Garden, the Silver and White Garden, the Woodland and Solar Wing Garden, the Cathedral Garden and many more. Decked out with plants and trees including roses, magnolia, azaleas, lilac, cherry plum and apple trees, rhododendrons, hedging, ferns, grapevines and a variety of vegetables, these gardens have been described by Alan Titchmarch as 'a tapestry of colourful blooms,' and they are a wonder to behold no matter what time of the year you chose to visit. There is also a moat pool, a pond, and a fantastic maze in the meadow close to the main entrance – brilliant for adults and children alike.

We now go back to 1463 (or thereabouts) when Cuthbert Billingham inherited the hall. After many years of residing at the house, Cuthbert and his wife went on a pilgrimage, leaving the house to his grandson John when he died. This was around the year 1508. After John's death in 1575 the hall went to Ralph Billingham and in 1615 the hall went to another Cuthbert Billingham – a descendant of the former Cuthbert Billingham. This Cuthbert Billingham caused quite a stir back in 1631 when he quarrelled with his mother and the good folk of Durham, resulting in Cuthbert cutting off their water supply. After a while, however, he was forced to turn it back on – much to his annoyance.

It is the niece of the fiery-tempered Mr Billingham who is said to haunt Crook Hall. Many a time she has been seen as she silently meanders through the hall. Known as the White Lady, the ghost of Crook Hall has been known to walk the premises for many years now, causing much interest for paranormal investigators and psychical researchers. There are a number of areas where the elusive phantom has been seen with the last recorded sighting being not that long ago. More often than not her presence is felt, rather than seen, around the hall. However, the best time (but not the only time) to see her is, by all accounts, on 20 December (St Thomas's Eve), when she is said to silently make her way down an ancient wooden and unused stairwell that is housed in the circular turret of the Jacobean manor house.

During my visit I met the owners Maggie and Keith Bell and spoke in great detail to Keith about their ghosts. He told me quite a bit in regards to their resident spectre. Keith showed me where exactly in the house she had been seen, which included the old stairwell and the medieval hall. Keith then diverted my attention to a notice on the wall near to where the old stairwell is situated that tells the visitor all about the White Lady. With kind permission from Keith and Maggie, I am able to reproduce the notice herein:

These ancient stairs, perhaps the oldest in County Durham, are haunted by the White Lady. She was the Niece of Cuthbert Billingham, who inherited Crook Hall in 1615. He quarrelled with the citizens of Durham and in his rage, cut off their water supply. There have been numerous sightings of the White Lady over the centuries. She is usually said to glide silently

The ancient stairwell at Crook Hall. It is here on 20 December (and other occasions) that the ghost of a lady in a flowing gown has been seen floating down the stairs.

and gently down the stairs, although on one occasion, she was reported to thoroughly alarm guests who had been invited to Crook Hall for a ball by a rather more dramatic appearance. A banquet had been laid out in the medieval hall, but as the guests moved into the Screen's Passage, they heard a soft rustle followed by a loud crash. When they looked into the hall they found that the tables had been overturned, destroying the banquet. A further rustle and a glimpse of a white figure convinced them that this was the work of the White Lady.

A wonderful anecdote of the Crook Hall ghost, and one wonders why she chose to ruin the party, after all, she is usually such a benign soul. I also had a 'strange experience' during my visit to the old house. I had been looking around the lower sections of the house and gardens for about an hour or so and had decided to venture upstairs and have a look around in the upper levels of the Jacobean manor house. It is in this part of the building where two rocking chairs (that are situated near to the balcony that overlooks the medieval hall) have been seen to move ever so gently back and forth when no one is near them.

The rocking chairs at Crook Hall, which have been seen to gently sway back and forth as though occupied by invisible people, though no one is anywhere near them.

The adjacent room is a large room with a wooden floor and it was in this room where I experienced something odd. I went inside for a look and noticed there was a toilet, so I decided to pay a quick visit. During my time in the lavatory I heard the distinct sound of footsteps as they made their way across the wooden floor, each footfall as crystal clear as the one preceding it. They began quite loud and quietened as they became further away. This made me assume that someone had come in the room and ventured over to the window to look out. When I came out of the toilet, I half expected to see another visitor to the house standing at the window as I had not heard the footfalls make their return journey back across the room. When I opened the door I found that I was in the room on my own! I looked around to see if anyone else was on the upper level with me and found no one around at all. Whoever had walked across the room to the window had stopped there and walked no further.

This is the first time I have relayed my experience from Crook Hall; in fact, I never even mentioned it to Maggie or Keith on the day of my visit. Why? I don't know to be honest; perhaps it was because I am getting so used to experiencing such things that I am taking them for granted. I am in haunted properties every chance I get so it's not surprising that I experience these strange things. I will leave the last word to Keith and Maggie to whom we all owe our thanks for keeping the spirit of Crook Hall alive and well for all to see:

Crook Hall.

Most of England's large city gardens have disappeared, so to have a hall and gardens, only a few hundred yards from the centre of a city, is a rarity. We believe you will be enchanted by your visit to Crook Hall and it is a restful contrast to the busy lives that we all lead. Whether you have visited before, or are returning once again, we hope you will enjoy your experience as every day seems magical in these atmospheric surroundings.

The Ghosts of Neville's Cross

On 17 October in the year of 1346, one of the most famous battles of the North-East took place: the Battle of Neville's Cross. On the moors that lie to the west of Durham City, close to Neville's Cross, two armies gathered to fight to the death. A Scottish army led by David II had invaded England at the command of the French king, Philip VI. This strategic plan was an effort to divert the English from their campaign in France at that time. It was a campaign they were seemingly going to emerge victorious from.

As the Scots advanced into England they destroyed many buildings whilst taking others, such as Lanercost Priory. After negotiating the Pennines, they arrived at Hexham and caused

Neville's Cross.

havoc and mayhem there, taking Hexham Priory in the process. They then made a beeline east to Durham. On 16 October 1346 the Scottish army arrived on the outskirts of Durham City and camped near an area where Bear Park is now located. Ten miles away from the Scots camp there gathered an English army that had been assembled by Ralph de Neville and Henry Percy.

After a pre-battle encounter between a number of Scottish soldiers and the English, the Scottish soldiers retreated back to their main camp to warn the rest of their throng, but it was too late. The English, by then, had reached the most favourable location in which to do battle from, which was on a narrow ridge on the outskirts of Neville's Cross itself. This resulted in the annihilation of the Scottish army as they found themselves at a severe disadvantage due to the poor fighting ground they found themselves on. Essentially they were defenceless from the English sub-army of first-rate archers that were perched high on the hillsides. It was these archers that crippled the Scots before they had a chance to even begin. The arrows were fired, swords were then viciously thrust into the chests of the Scots, and axes were wielded that hacked them to pieces and the Neville's Cross massacre continued until the land was saturated in the warm blood of 20,000 men.

Eventually, after hours of fighting, the Scots fled the field leaving their king in the hands of the English. The English had terminated the invasion from the North and the Scots that fled were sent packing back to the borderlands.

Crossgate Moor Panoramic – the actual battle site of Neville's Cross in 1346, and stretching as far as the eye can see. It is also known as the Red Hills.

On a day trip to visit and photograph the site of the battlefield in May 2009 I stumbled across something that I was previously unaware of. Walking along a stretch of thoroughfare called Toll House Road, which leads from Neville's Cross to Bear Park (which takes you straight through Crossgate Moor, the site of the battle) I discovered – quite by chance – a tale of mystery and intrigue. I came across two local ramblers and asked them where the best place was to take a picture of the battle site. I was informed the best view of the entire area was from the blue footbridge on the main road close to Neville's Cross (which was a mile or so from where I had just come from).

I said my thanks and bid the ramblers farewell. Just as I was heading back off to take my photographs, one of the hikers turned around and called out to me. He went on to tell me about an old stone bridge that lay about a quarter of a mile down the lane where, local tradition has it, the Scottish king fled and hid for a while before his imminent capture by the English. The odd thing about this was that, according to the ramblers, the bridge was also supposedly haunted. Now, I had never mentioned to these hikers why I was in the area, so I can safely assume that they were not having me on. (If I had told them I was researching a ghost book it may have been a different story.)

The walker also said some people believe that, on the anniversary of the battle, you could actually hear the cries and the sighs of the trembling king as he cowers under the stone arch

Aldin Grange Bridge situated between Neville's Cross and Bear Park. It was under this bridge that the Scottish king, David, supposedly hid after running from the English.

fearing for his life. I am not sure how much truth there is in this tale; in fact, the story of the king hiding out there in the first place is based only on local legend, so no one knows for sure if he really did conceal himself there. Maybe he did, maybe legend has it wrong – I guess we will never know for certain. One thing is sure, however; I deemed this account interesting enough for it to find its way into these pages. The single stone arched bridge in question is called Aldin Grange Bridge and it lies at the bottom of a little valley with the River Browney running under it. I found the bridge and took a number of photographs for my records. It is a beautiful area of Crossgate Moor and I could have spent the entire day there basking in the glorious sunshine.

In regards to the actual battle, well…over 650 years later the echoes of that horrific day are still said to be seen and heard, as the battle is purportedly re-enacted in spectral form. Some claim to have seen the ghosts of the soldiers as they do battle for the umpteenth time – only ever so silently. Others claim to have heard only the deafening roar of the soldiers clashing with each other. Legend has it that if you were to walk around the actual Neville's Cross nine times, and then put your ear to the ground, you would hear the unmistakable sound of the battle that once took place there.

There is another sad and tragic tale associated with this area, and this comes in the form of one of Durham's many 'grey ladies'. This phantom is also connected to the Battle of Neville's Cross in the respect that the woman in question was said to be the wife of a soldier who had

This stone marker was erected to commemorate the Battle of Neville's Cross. It stands surrounded by a metal fence with spear-pointed tips – how appropriate.

been killed on that fateful day back in 1346. The ghost is thought to be searching for her lost husband. She is said to have told him that if he enrolled for the battle she would leave him forever but he felt too patriotic and signed up nonetheless. After his death she was so racked with remorse that she died of a broken heart and subsequently haunts the area in search of her husband, perhaps to let him know she has forgiven him.

In days of yore, prior to the advent of the motorcar, people would have to travel using shank's pony. If they were lucky, or if they had a few bob (a 'few bob' is a tem used in the North-East for money), they would ride on horse and cart. Those who rode on horse and cart and travelled up Crossgate Peth (close to Neville's Cross) often reported strange sightings of another ghost woman. More often than not, during their ride, they would suddenly discover that they had somehow picked up a mysterious hitchhiker, for across from where they sat upon their carts – or carriages – they would see a solemn looking lady dressed in grey and holding an infant in her arms. She would usually sit in the cart/carriage, remaining ever so silent and forlorn, until it reached the area that is Neville's Cross at the top of the bank. Then the figure would fade away into the ether.

In modern times, however, the phantom grey lady has been seen less and less. Perhaps due to the lack of horse-drawn carriages? There is yet another ghost woman who is seen in this area. She is believed to be the spectre of a murder victim from Victorian times. After being thrown down a flight of stairs by a soldier who is alleged to have confessed to the crime, the woman has been seen flitting about the area. Some people think that this woman may well be the shade of the soldier's wife of Neville's Cross, but the fact that the phantom is seen without infant indicates otherwise. So it appears there are a number of sad ghosts of women in this vicinity, stalking the area forever in their endless quest for peace. Do let me know if you see them.

The Manor House

The Manor House lies roughly on the edge of the City of Durham. In the sixteenth century, when first erected, the building served as a farmhouse. In 1642, a certain John Wilkinson sold it to one John Shawe, and when Shawe died ownership passed to his grandson, Ralph. By the early 1700s, the house and surrounding land had been through a succession of owners.

However, by 1885 only the house remained as the land had been sold on to a local colliery. In 1891 the building was fully renovated and subsequently occupied by a man called Henry Palmer. Since Palmer's death it has been rented and/or owned by many other occupants. In 2001 a family bought the premises and turned the Manor House into a thriving hotel, which is still open to this day.

This sixteenth-century one-time orphanage, manor house and now hotel is reputedly haunted by a number of ghosts and spirits that once had some connection with the locality. The spectre of a woman is said to amble along the stairwell looking for her child. Those who have seen her claim that she looks anguished. It is also said that the bones of several youngsters were found buried in the grounds adjacent to the house, leading some researchers to hint at the possibility of murder. Rooms 7 and 8 have also been subjected to extremely aggressive poltergeist-like activity and spectral apparitions have, on occasion, resulted in terrifying the present owners.

After a well-known television ghost investigation team had shot an episode there, and after another North-East paranormal research team had come to investigate, the problems at the property seemed to become a whole lot worse for the owners. After this, the Manor House was 'shut down' to investigative teams, as it seemed that the intrusion and interference were making matters worse. Two exorcisms were, at different times, carried out on the premises and

The landing at the Manor House Hotel in Ferryhill is said to be haunted by a spectral woman looking for her child.

both exorcists claimed they had rid the hotel of their unwelcome visitor – they had not. Some time elapsed and eventually another research team – a team with morals, principles and ethics – were allowed in to see if they could document any of the paranormal phenomena. The team that was allowed in to investigate was one of the leading ghost-hunting teams in the region and a team that had (and still has) good credentials – GHOST.

A good friend of mine, and fellow ghost hunter, Fiona Vipond, was at the time, and still is to my knowledge, very good friends with the owner of the Manor House and it is thanks to Fiona that the Ghosts and Hauntings Overnight Surveillance Team were allowed access to the property to carry out their investigations. It was a few years ago now that we spent the night there in search of its resident ghosts and we all experienced, much to our surprise and delight, some wonderful, odd phenomena during our stay. For our investigation we were assigned the two most haunted rooms in the hotel, rooms 7 and 8 and the corridors. This was where most of the aforementioned phenomena had taken place and as we prepared for the night's investigations, we wondered just what (if anything) was in store for us.

During the course of our investigation we noted a few unusual temperature drops, and one or two electromagnetic readings (EMFs) were ascertained. In room 7 it was found that our trigger object, a cross, had been moved from its original position, but our best results of the night came from room 8. The evil entity that has caused so much trouble for the owners and their family, and which allegedly resides in this room, did not make his presence known to us that night but we truly believe that the lost spirits of two children did.

What happened in that room on that night was one of the finest examples of what we believe to be spirit interaction with 'the flour tray experiment' in all of our investigations to date. Before we go any further, let me just explain what a flour tray experiment is: the investigators half-fill a tray, or a flat container, with flour. After the flour is flattened out, objects or bits and pieces that are relevant to the alleged spirits are placed firmly into the flour in the hope that whatever spirit is said to reside there will interact with it (for example, a cross is used if the ghost is said to be a monk or a nun, coins are used if the ghost is supposed to be a smuggler, or toys, perhaps, if the ghosts are children). The tray is then left on a flat surface like a bench or a shelf where you know it won't be disturbed, either on purpose or by accident during the investigation. If you find the flour disturbed or the objects have moved in what must be a controlled environment, you may have achieved physical spiritual interaction.

Before we attempted a séance we placed down a flour tray on the sideboard and, prior to turning the lights off, we took a photograph of it. It showed ten crystals, a red lollipop, and flat, undisturbed floor. The rest of the group sat in the circle for the séance while Drew Bartley and I monitored the proceedings from the sidelines. When everyone was ready and comfortable, Suzanne Hitchinson proceeded to conduct the séance and it wasn't long before she was aware of spirit presences. She picked up on two children, a boy and a girl, and said they were related. Fiona Vipond then asked the alleged spirit children if they would like a lollipop. Fiona then said that they were welcome to take the lollipop we had left as a trigger object in the flour (little did we know what effect Fiona's offer would have).

After a minute or so, I shone my torch onto the flour tray to see if there had been any movement with our objects and I was not disappointed. I noticed that the flour had indeed been disturbed, as if someone had dragged two or three of their fingers through the flour, leaving it piled up at one side of the tray; this flour had seriously been disturbed! But the real

Room 8 of the Manor House, where the author and his colleagues experienced some of the most bewildering paranormal phenomena they have ever seen.

shock came when we all noticed that the red lollipop had completely vanished from within the tray. It must be stressed that I was in fact monitoring the séance from that very area so I know that no one had touched it. Drew Bartley was on the other side of the room, and everyone else was sitting in the séance – and holding hands. So who took the lollipop? It is not hard to work out that it must have been one of the spirit children.

This was a first for us all, for all the flour tray experiments we have set up over the years. Granted, some do indeed move from their positions, but only slightly or an inch at the most, but this one had completely vanished and was taken away from under our noses. I can assure you that no one touched that flour tray and everyone turned out their pockets and was checked for flour on their hands and clothes, just as a precautionary measure. Everyone was clean, but I knew that this would be the case. It is also interesting to add that a patch of flour and flour stains were later found on the carpet near the room door, (this patch was the identical size and shape of the lollipop); we also found traces of flour in the bathroom, outside on the landing and down the stairs in the corridor.

We can only conclude that it was taken from the flour tray by the children said to haunt this area, out of the actual room, into the corridor and down the stairs. We all know that no one living had actually left the room while we were in there. This incident baffled us all somewhat, and we were convinced that we had experienced true ghostly activity. We were so impressed, we spent the rest of the night talking it through and trying to locate the lollipop stick. We never found it.

NOTE: It must now be stressed that since our visit in 2005 the activity and the spiritual trouble that the premises has experienced have depleted to the point of non-existence, much to the relief of the owners. Because of this, the owners will not let anyone else in to re-investigate as the thought of stirring something back up concerns them somewhat. It had taken over four years for whatever was residing in there to 'calm down' so please, when visiting the premises show some respect for both the property owners and the entity.

The Dancing Spook of Shincliffe Peth

To most people, ghosts and hauntings, spectres and ghouls can be very frightening if you are ever unlucky enough to come across them. The vast majority of the time, however, sightings of these 'visitors from beyond', and activity that is thought to be either active spirits, or even poltergeist phenomena, can be easily explained away. When a paranormal investigator gets to work on a case they should really be seeking out the normal explanations as opposed to the paranormal one. I think this is where the problems lie with a lot of ghost hunters out there as they are all too eager to believe that whatever they experience on vigils are ghosts making themselves known.

It is so easy to venture into a so-called haunted property full of expectations as to what may happen during the course of the investigation, and so when naturally occurring 'things' begin to happen they are mistakenly taken for paranormal phenomena. I have seen this happen hundreds of times during my years of research and it always pains me to point out that the creaking that had just been heard is due to the floorboards contracting and stretching as the property is settling down for the night. Another example is when overexcited investigators find 'orbs' on their pictures and cry out 'we have activity!' I have done enough study into hauntings now to realise that these so-called 'spiritual spots' of light are nothing more than reflections of dust particles that are hanging in the air. Misinterpretation of phenomena can easily occur and one has to be so careful if they decide to take on the role of ghost hunter. I have made these errors myself on occasions, so I am not making myself out to be the exception, on the contrary, but we have to remember that mistakes are there to be learned from and if we don't learn from past errors, we will hardly move forward within this field of endeavour.

This brings me nicely on to a classic ghost tale that frightened residents of Durham City to the extent that they needed the police to solve the problem. It was back in 1926 when locals witnessed 'the dancing spook of Shincliffe Peth,' but after much debate about what was actually going on, the mystery was eventually solved. Shincliffe Peth is a stretch of road that is rather steep to say the least, and it leads from Durham City to Shincliffe. It is flanked with deep woodland either side of it and so it was the ideal locale for the ghost. The ghost was first seen by a group of walkers who were making their way home one evening after spending time in the city. As they made their approach to the steep gradient, they were astonished to see in the distance a weird shape, dancing around in front of them, accompanied by the harrowing sounds of rattling chains, and screeching.

This spectacle was about 100 metres away from the crowd, and considering it was dusk, their visibility was quite poor; all they could see and hear was something strange hovering above the lane, dancing around and making 'woo' noises like a stereotypical ghost would do. They made a hasty retreat to the top of the hill and subsequently discussed, in terror, what it was they were seeing. Personally I think it is rather hard to believe that a group of grown individuals were actually frightened by this…rattling chains and woo noises! But as mentioned earlier on, if you believe in ghosts, and are thrown into a situation where you think you may be encountering one, your mind begins to work overtime and the fear soon takes hold. Whatever it was on Shincliffe Peth somehow had the desired effect. Of course fear, they say, is infectious, and when one person becomes frightened it has a knock-on effect and in this case the whole group, bar one, became so terrified that they would not venture down the lane to go home.

Luckily, one of the group was part of the Durham Constabulary, and although he was admittedly somewhat scared, he had the courage to investigate. After a short while he decided to venture down the lane alone to see if he could get to the bottom of the strange occurrences that had just been witnessed. Upon reaching the area where the ghost was seen, he found, to his amusement, that a white sheet had been precariously placed upon a coat hanger, which in turn was suspended from overhanging trees. With the aid of strings that led into the woods, the spook was found to have been manipulated by a group of youths that had hidden in the trees. Upon the arrival of the policeman, the pranksters fled into the night leaving the apparition to be cut down by the officer, who then made his way back up the hill and showed all his terrified friends…much to their relief.

I do love this tale, as it really is funny. You can just imagine the group of tricksters running off into the night, falling about laughing, knowing they have scared the living daylights out of some would-be passers by. I think a newspaper reporter found it rather amusing too as the account ended up in one of the local dailies back in September of 1926. This 'ghost story' (that is what it is) does, however, illustrate the point that I made previously, and that is that not everything you see and hear in spooky areas, or indeed, in haunted houses, are what you perceive them to be.

The Crooked Spectre of North Bailey

The North and South Bailey are areas of Durham that are nicely tucked away behind the magnificent castle and cathedral. They are in the midst of the most remarkable and attractive streets in the city and have been described by the architectural historian Sir Nikolaus Bernhard Leon Pevsner CBE (1902-1983) as 'the best streets in Durham.' In times gone by, the houses in these parts of Durham were of great significance, as they were said to have been occupied by military and police personnel who were specifically employed to protect the city from various kinds of assault.

One of the houses in North Bailey – I am not sure which, but some suggest a property that was once owned by the city's chief constable – is said to be the home to the friendly spectre of an old man. He has reportedly been seen coming out from a cellar wearing a dirty and worn white shirt, a pair of black trousers and a cap. This frail old gent hobbles around as if he is in some pain and is said to be hunched over and all twisted up. Perhaps this old chap was riddled

North Bailey is said to be home to the friendly spectre of an old man. He has been seen emerging from the cellar of one of these houses, wearing a dirty and worn white shirt, a pair of black trousers and a cap.

with arthritis when he was alive and his crippled ghost now lurches and staggers around for all eternity. This brings one thought to mind – psychics and spirit mediums are forever telling us that when an individual passes over into the spirit world they leave all their physical disabilities and ailments behind, entering the spirit world ailment free. Now if this is the case, why do we have reports of headless ghosts, or see spectres with limps as they drag their injured leg behind them when they walk? Perhaps the stone tape theory holds more validity than we think. There are, however, cases where the active spirit is said to have had a speech impediment or damaged lungs for example, as they have been either heard to talk strangely or gasp for breath.

To my knowledge the crooked spectre of North Bailey has only been seen on a few occasions, a very long time ago. It is also a mystery who he is, and why he haunts the area. It is said that the crooked spectre is not the only residing ghost in this area. Spectral school children dressed in old-fashioned uniforms have been seen in this area, along with a musician and an unknown and mysterious woman. It seems to me that this street is awash with ghosts.

Langley Old Hall Ruin

The ruin of Langley Old Hall is on the outskirts of Durham City and is situated on a knoll overlooking the River Browney. It is one of the city's hidden gems but very little of it remains, bar a ruined and quite dangerous curtain wall that is hidden in a copse of trees. The building is said to have been one of the larger and more prominent halls in Durham but remains somewhat unfamiliar to most Durham folk due to the aforementioned facts.

This one-time fortified Tudor house stood dominating the surrounding land and, according to one of the North-East's most highly regarded historians, David Simpson, 'the house was more like a castle than a hall, which was associated with members of the powerful Scrope family.' They remained there until the hall fell into a serious state of disrepair in the 1750s. The site of the house has remained in this very unstable condition since. It must be noted that the site of this former home is now very much inaccessible, with the remaining ruin being in danger of collapsing. My advice is don't go snooping around, for obvious reasons.

During its heyday the hall is said to have had a magnificent gravelled drive that led from the main road to the house and it is this driveway that is said to be haunted by a phantom coach and four. Observed by numerous folk thundering towards the ruined hall, the coach in question is said to be pulled by four jet black – and headless – horses. As with the usual horse and coach phantoms, the spectral coach is said to disappear at the top of the drive. Sometimes, allegedly, only the sound of the wheels and the horses' hooves are heard as they make their way over the gravel.

Personally I am inclined to think that this ghost legend is just that, a legend. As there are a number of versions of the story (one suggesting that the coach and four is part of a funeral procession), with nothing being found in the records to verify anything, we can only take this account of a haunting as a spine-chilling anecdote.

An artist's impression of the 'headless horses and ghost coach' that has been seen making its way up the old drive to Langley Old Hall ruins. (Illustration by Julie Olley)

Vane Tempest Hall

Vane Tempest Hall is situated in the Gilesgate area of Durham City and is currently used as a community centre. In the past, however, it was known as the Gilesgate Militia Barracks. According to my fellow investigator and good friend Cindy Nunn, a genealogist, paranormal expert and historian:

> No one knows for sure when Vane Tempest Hall was actually built but according to some local sources there are two possibilities. The first suggests it was built in 1851 and used by the Durham military until it was converted into a Community Association Centre. The second version suggests that Vane Tempest Hall is the only remaining militia headquarters that is Grade II listed in County Durham. Built in 1863 as the 2nd Durham Militia Stores, it is an impressive sandstone building in mock castle style.

Cindy has noted that 'there is a stone carving on the building which brings us closer to 1863 being the actual build date, and beginning of use probably 1865.' The majestic Vane Tempest Hall has a chequered history dating back to the 1860s. Since then it has been home to a number of army units and has even doubled up as a hospital. At one time the barracks' stables were used as a smallpox hospital, which included a 'dead room' for storing deceased bodies. As can be expected, this area is considered to be extremely haunted and many have reported paranormal experiences while working in the buildings.

Vane Tempest Hall in Gilesgate, where Colin and Cindy Nunn of API encountered many odd occurrences during their investigations. The venue is reputed to house a number of ghosts. (Courtesy of Cindy and Colin Nunn)

The plaque on the wall indicating when Vane Tempest Hall may have been built. (Courtesy of Cindy and Colin Nunn)

The parade grounds are said to be haunted by a militia soldier who accidentally blew himself up by a cannon while shooting it on the parade grounds. Those who have seen his spectre have found it to be an upsetting experience. On the other side of the barracks' wall is an ancient burial ground. Accounts of a 'white lady' floating through the wall and walking the parade grounds have been made by a number of people.

Cindy and her team, Anomalous Phenomena Investigations (API) have spent much time investigating Vane Tempest Hall and have spent many a night inside the premises conducting scientific tests to see if they could ascertain any paranormal phenomena.

Cindy has told me that on her investigations there a number of odd paranormal incidences occurred. One night (29 July 2006) during a vigil in the sports hall area, which, incidentally, was the former Epidemic Hospital area, also known as the aforementioned 'dead room', whispering voices were heard during an experiment with some dowsing rods. No one was around to account for these 'whisperings' and, more oddly still, they seemed to be coming from within the room where the dowsing experiments were taking place.

Numerous cold spots and notable temperature drops were observed too by the team. During the vigils it was reported that 'a cold, heavy air brushes against Cindy's left arm.' Kevin (another investigator) also felt the cold air. 'A cold spot is felt between Kevin and Cindy for about thirty seconds and then suddenly the air rapidly warms up.' Cindy further explained:

At 8.49 p.m., I attempted to take some photos and managed to get only two shots before the Fuji A101 camera jammed before going dead. The batteries were fully charged when they were inserted just prior to the start of the vigil. At 8:51 p.m., I replaced the camera batteries with new ones. Whilst doing so the team heard a door open and close somewhere in the building. Colin and Kevin went to investigate but found nothing to account for the noises we had just heard. Later on in the investigation, when we were staking out the Reception area of the premises, we all [Colin Nunn, Sharon Brentnall and Cindy Nunn] heard the sound of a door handle being rattled down the hall near the base room, as if someone (or something) was trying to open a door. This occurred after I had encouraged any spirit presence to make itself known to us.

So, it seems that Vane Tempest Hall may well be haunted after all. I asked if there was any sign of the infamous white lady or the militia soldier during their investigations there and was told, 'unfortunately not yet, but we do have plans to return, so you never know…'

Dryburn – The Site of Executions

One cannot write a book about the ghosts of Durham City without mentioning the area where the public executions once took place – the site of the Dryburn Gallows. Many a time during my visits to Durham the bus that I was travelling on – the number 21 from Newcastle – would pass this area *en route*. Little did I realise at the time that the area where the County Hall and Dryburn hospital is was the area in which the gallows were located up until the year 1816. After 1816 the hangings were of course held outside Durham Jail when the new 'long drop' system came into place. This was to give the prisoners a swifter, less painful death.

There are two explanations as to why the area is called Dryburn. Rumour has it that after a priest was hung on the gallows, the local burn or river that once ran through there mysteriously dried up, as if a drought had occurred. It has remained dry since that time. Others believe that the word Dryburn is derived from the word 'Tyburn', which of course was a place known for execution in York on the Knavesmire, and in London, near Marylebone.

Like most gallows sites people were brought there to be killed for crimes such as theft, burglary, treason, murder and of course witchcraft. Justice was tough and was carried out swiftly so if someone was accused of breaking the law and being a wrongdoer, it wouldn't be long before they were a lifeless corpse swaying in the breeze. On one occasion it is said that five people were hung by the necks until they were dead simply because people thought they were gypsies – talk about rough justice.

In regards to ghosts, well…they say the area is not haunted. If it is haunted then the authorities must have kept it quiet. You would think that at a place which has seen so much death, misery, anguish and pain there would be one or two ghosts, but to my knowledge and much to my disappointment there isn't. Having said that, maybe there really aren't any ghosts near to the site of the old gallows. A lot of ghosts that return from the grave are said to haunt the areas where they were once happy in life, at home or with loved ones. Whether the area is 'spooked out' or not I guess we will never know for sure, and does it really matter? The site is inaccessible anyway so we can't just go wandering in there; besides, if there are ghosts I am sure we will hear about them one day.

Dryburn – the site of execution. A marker stands on the very spot where the Durham gallows once stood. An inscription reads, 'Dryburn – No doubt the priests were martyrs before god, by George Swallowell 1590'.

At the top of North Road, at the far end of the roundabout, which is opposite the County Hall offices, stands a small but poignant reminder of those barbaric days of olde. A relatively new, but long awaited, stone memorial stands proudly to honour priests who gave their lives for the memory of those who died on the Dryburn gallows.

Although this area doesn't seem to be haunted, the one place where we will find a spirit or two lurking is, of course, the local pub. And that is where we will head off now, for a pint of fine ale and a friendly chat with landlords and landladies alike about their pubs' resident spirits (and I mean the ethereal kind). Just be sure, from this day on, to look at whichever drinking den or alehouse you choose to visit in Durham City with fresh eyes. Not all of the customers in the bar may be visible to the naked eye, and if the manager looks to be dead upon his feet…who knows? Maybe he really is…

two

DURHAM'S HAUNTED
PUBS AND INNS

Jimmy Allen's

We begin our ghost tour of Durham's pubs and inns with a visit to one of the finest bars in the city – where one of the most famous spectres of Durham resides. Built in around 1632, and tucked away under Elvet Bridge, is a building that was once used as a 'house of correction' and the offices for the *Durham Chronicle*, of course not at the same time. Nowadays the building is more commonly known as Jimmy Allen's pub and is named after the ghost that is said to haunt the building.

There are, it seems, two ghost stories relating to the one ghost at Jimmy Allen's, with noticeable differences. The first story declares that the ghost is that of a piper who was brought to the area via a severe flood. Apparently, he was caught up in the floodwaters and washed a few miles down river where he was subsequently pulled from the River Wear near Elvet Bridge. For some reason, he was labelled a wrongdoer and was locked away in the house of correction until he died a natural death some months later. His ghost is said to be heard playing the very pipes that he was hauled from the 'in-spate' river with, in the lower area of the pub around midnight which, of course, was the old prison.

In the second story, the phantom has been given a name, that of Jimmy Allen. Jimmy Allen is said to have been the official Northumbrian piper to the Duchess of Northumberland and, for the last seven years of his life, for crimes such as hustling and theft, he spent it locked up in a cell there. Initially Jimmy was sentenced to death for his crimes but his sentence was later reduced to life imprisonment by the Prince Regent. However, fate would deal him a vicious blow for his sentence was only commuted the day after he was executed in 1810.

As with the first tale, it is said that if you listen carefully you can hear the ghost of Jimmy Allen playing gently on his Northumbrian pipes, the melodic sounds reverberating around the

Jimmy Allen's bar tucked away under Elvet Bridge..

A photograph of Elvet Bridge and Bridge House from 1900. Jimmy Allen's is situated to the left of the picture on the other side of the Wear. (Courtesy of Newcastle Libraries and Information Service)

OLD HOUSE ON ELVET BRIDGE, DURHAM.182

old lower levels of this one-time gaol-house. Whatever tale you choose to believe (if any) the fact remains that the old pub does indeed retain a certain 'atmosphere' within its walls. With ghost stories, you often get a number of different versions, as we have seen in this instance. Over time, little details can be forgotten with new bits woven into the narrative leaving the story not as true as one would like to think. Had it not been for the following incident, I may have been inclined to think that the legend of the ghost of Jimmy Allen's was nothing more than that, a legend. Let me explain.

The Ghosts and Haunting Overnight Surveillance Team, which I co-founded in January 2005, spent an uneventful night there a few years ago, investigating the haunting with nothing much happening at all in the way of paranormal phenomena. I could not attend the investigation due to other ghost-hunting commitments but by all accounts, I did not miss much. However, two other co-founders and colleagues of mine from the investigative team, Drew Bartley and Fiona Vipond, had visited the bar prior to the team's overnight investigation and had been shown around the place by the duty manager. They were fully aware of the pub's reputation and subsequently asked if they could see the areas that were once used as the holding cells on the lower levels. This, of course, is where the phantom piper is allegedly seen and heard. The duty manager kindly obliged and so the old cellars were visited.

During the course of this visit they spent a total of ten to fifteen minutes in the lower area of the building, taking pictures and generally seeing if they could 'snap' anything of a paranormal nature. Little did they know that they were about to photograph one of the strangest images they have ever seen. When looking back at the pictures (while still in the cellar area) Fiona was astounded to notice a figure. This figure was in the centre of the frame near to the back of the passageway, and it looked as though it was hooded. The next picture showed nothing at all nor did the picture that was taken prior to the anomalous one. The figure on the image does indeed look like a hooded individual, perhaps a monk, and analysis of the picture indicates that whatever occurred was within the picture, and not a camera malfunction.

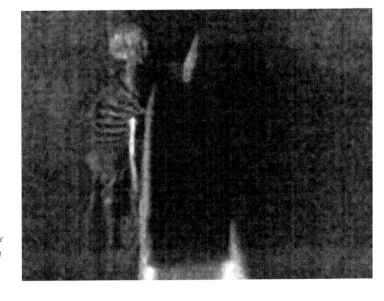

The photograph of what is believed to be a monk taken by Fiona Vipond on an impromptu visit to Jimmy Allen's one night with fellow ghost hunter, Drew Bartley. (Note – the skeleton in the picture is a plastic model.) (Courtesy of Fiona Vipond)

Tests were carried out at the time to see if any of the clutter that was held down there could account for the shape that was photographed – it could not. More pictures were taken to try and reproduce the image to see if there was a normal explanation after all, yet no matter how many times they took pictures, the monk-like figure did not return. The bar staff who were there with Drew and Fiona became very frightened and excited, with one of them making a sharp exit from the cellars after seeing the picture. To this day the image remains a mystery and one can't help thinking that Drew and Fiona may very well have caught an image of the ghost of Jimmy Allen's.

The Black Horse Inn

You could say a haunted pub is like good single malt: they both mature with age. The Black Horse Inn at Durham has only been known to be haunted since the 1970s, despite the fact that the building has stood for almost two centuries. The ghost that is said to reside there, as announced by the (then) residents of the inn, was thought to be a poltergeist. Nowadays of course it is more commonly thought by 'serious researchers' that poltergeists and ghosts are not actually the same thing, with poltergeists being 'psychic' as opposed to being 'spiritual'. (See *The South Shields Poltergeist* – Hallowell and Ritson, 2008.)

By all accounts a number of inexplicable occurrences took place at the pub, such as newly fitted light bulbs falling from the sockets on the ceiling and breaking with a crash upon the pub floor. The landlady recalled that on one occasion two bulbs fell to the floor within seconds of one another. Having swept up the shattered bulb glass, it was reported by another witness that pieces of the actual bulb, that moments earlier she had swept away, had mysteriously returned to the very spot where she had just swept them from – most peculiar.

An artist's impression of the 'terrified girl' as she runs from her room in the Black Horse pub after waking to see the hooded figure of a man standing by her bed. (Illustration by Julie Olley)

During the research for this book, I also discovered, with the help of Mike Hallowell, that electric fires housed at the pub had a strange tendency to 'behave in a most unreliable manner', as Hallowell puts it. This phenomenon was just the beginning of the story as other things deemed strange were experienced there too. I was informed that alarm clocks began to ring incessantly throughout the night, keeping the household awake and, more chillingly, a young teenage girl ran from her bedroom in sheer terror one night claiming that there was a man standing over her bed who was 'wearing a strange robe'.

There was supposedly a woman pushed down the stairs to her death in the pub many years before these incidents, so could she be responsible for the activity? The thought occurs that the activity could have come about by the teenager who resided there at the time, after all, they are the stereotypical, and more often than not, unwitting focuses for poltergeist activity.

The Market Tavern

The Market Tavern inn is located in the mrket square and dates back to the sixteenth century. It is in a prime spot in the centre of the busy market place and is popular with locals, tourists, shoppers and students. This fine city centre drinking establishment is adorned with old oak beams, has a polished wooden floor, and an abundance of old and framed black-and-white prints dating back many years. It sells real pub grub, and some of the best hand-pulled ales in the region. I found myself visiting the Market Tavern (which was originally named the City Tavern) time and time again during my visits to Durham when deciding to either grab a spot of lunch, or just enjoy some liquid refreshment – ah the joys of ghost researching.

I discovered, during a chat with a staff member, that the pub's popularity was ensured after an Act of Parliament in 1851 which allowed meat, fish and poultry to be sold in the square where the pub stands. This area subsequently became a focal point of Durham City. Two years later, in 1853, it was declared by the Council Committee of Durham (CCD) that the water supply that was generated from a nearby source to supply that particular area was unsuitable for human consumption.

The Market Tavern pub in the market square, which is said to be haunted by two ghosts.

Durham market place in 1920. The building behind the rear seat of the old car is in fact now the Market Tavern.
(Courtesy of Newcastle Libraries and Information Service)

This, in turn, left the Market Tavern the only place available for a drink. The alehouse couldn't have been located in a better place.

I also discovered that the pub lays claim to having a ghost, or two. No one is sure whether there really is a ghost residing there but the rumours do indeed persist. One ghost is thought to be that of a knight who has been heard to clank and clink around in the cellar of the inn. The other ghost is said to be that of a nice old lady who also haunts the cellar. I also heard that the two ghosts at the inn are, in actual fact, really the same ghost with two different interpretations of what they are. But how can anyone get an old woman and a knight confused with one another? Unless there really are two ghosts at the pub…do I confuse you?

Regardless of what or who haunts the inn, the individual I spoke to during one of my visits had never heard of the pub's ghost. When asked if they had ever experienced anything of a spooky nature while working there I was told 'no'. That's not to say there are no ghosts though. So what makes the author believe that the Market Tavern is worthy of being within the pages of this book? Well, I just happen to own an old newspaper clipping from March 1999 that reviews the inn and spills the beans about the alleged phantoms that reside within these ancient walls.

The Nicky Nack Pub / Field

The following account comes from another book that I researched and wrote with the aforementioned Mike Hallowell. It is a tale of fun and games that ultimately turns to horror with a macabre death, and a possible (but unlikely) manifestation of the Devil himself. Technically speaking, the story revolves around a nearby field that once shared its name with the inn. It is featured in this section of the book simply because the story is indeed pub related, as we shall see.

Harvest time is a gruelling season for farmers, and when the work is done labourers will often celebrate by supping a pint or two of ale. This tradition is an old one, and was kept up religiously in the village of Tudhoe in Durham.

Last century – or some say in the century before – a group of farmers gathered one evening in Tudhoe Mill farm with a generous amount of alcohol. Their work having been completed, they now had time to relax.

Late into the hours of darkness the ale started to run out, and a young farmhand was asked to go to the nearby village of Croxdale to gather fresh supplies from a local inn that was still open. A large jug of whisky had taken their fancy, and he promised to return promptly with exactly that.

An hour ticked by, then two, and still the farmhand had not returned. One of the others decided to play a trick on him by way of revenge for his delay. He took a white sheet and headed off for a nearby field that lay between Croxdale and Tudhoe.

'I'll dress up as a ghost and frighten the daylights out of him as he comes back across the field,' he had told his pals with a mischievous grin.

Another hour or two passed, and suddenly the first young man staggered through the door of the farmhouse looking petrified.

'I was passing through the field, when suddenly a white ghost jumped out and frightened me!' he stammered.

His friends laughed hysterically, knowing full well that the 'ghost' had merely been their other friend playing pranks. But the laughing soon stopped when the frightened youngster carried on speaking.

'The white ghost was bad enough, but when the black one appeared it was even worse.'

Now they were puzzled.

'What black ghost?'

'Well, it was bigger than the white ghost, and it fell on top of it. Then there were terrible screams, and they both disappeared into the night.'

Concerned, they all traipsed down to the field. All that remained was the shredded remnants of the white sheet, covered in blood. Their friend was never seen again.

One curious postscript to this tale is that the first worker to cross the field – the one who was supposed to be the victim of the ghostly prank – claimed that as he ran back to the farm, terrified, he could hear the Devil calling out to him, 'Knicky-Nack! Knicky-Nack!'

Later, this mystery was explained when it was found that the young man's heel had come loose and was making the 'nicky-nack' noise when it slapped against the road as he ran!

Later, the field was renamed the Nicky Nack Field and still bears that title to this day. The public house in Croxdale was also, for a time, renamed the Nicky Nack, although it now carries the slightly less curious name of the Daleside Arms.

The Shakespeare Tavern

This pub is the smallest pub I have ever seen in my life. It is located at 63 Saddler Street, which leads up from the market square to Durham Castle and the cathedral. The pub was named in days of olde when this particular area of Durham was known for its theatres. The pub has wooden floors and panelled walls and retains a charm and character that few pubs do. Pictures by the internationally renowned photographer Royston Thomas, who is a regular at the pub, festoon the walls along with olde world wall lights that give the small inn a really cosy and intimate feel. If a quiet pint in friendly surroundings is required then the Shakespeare Tavern is the place to go. This fine drinking establishment has three accolades, a) It is the smallest pub in Durham, b) it is the oldest pub in Durham, and c) it is reputedly the most haunted pub in Durham. Built in 1190 the building has experienced many years of history and therefore it has seen a lot of faces come and go. That is why the owners think the place is so haunted.

The smallest, yet 'most haunted' public house in Durham is thought to be the Shakespeare Tavern on Saddler Street. It is a quaint little drinking den with an olde world charm and character…and the ale is good too.

I spoke to the owner of the inn, Paddy Solan, who was more than happy to share his ghost stories with me. He informed me that he had had an experience of the paranormal whilst lying in his bed in the flat which is situated above the pub. He told me that after a hard night's work he retired to his bed and slept soundly throughout the night. It wasn't until the next morning when he was lying in his bed wide-awake that he felt someone, or something, sit on the bed behind him (he was laying on his side). He said that he was aware of the bed sinking down and felt as though whoever was there was sitting up against him as this feeling was observed too. He froze for a moment, as he knew that there was no one in the flat – or at least there shouldn't have been – before jumping out of bed to find no one in his room at all.

Paddy is a sceptical individual but is not arrogant enough to suggest there is absolutely nothing in it. On the contrary, he is an open-minded person and is quite objective about what goes on at the inn.

I asked him what other strange occurrences had been experienced at the pub and he told me that his wife, Irene, had encountered one of the pub's many ghosts not long after they had moved in, in November 2005. The pub was closed for a week so essential maintenance could be carried out and, during that time, builders were contracted to carry out some much-needed work. It was during this first week of their occupancy that Irene experienced her first brush with the paranormal.

She had popped upstairs to the flat and heard some loud and distinct footfalls coming from nearby as she made her way along the passageway. Thinking it was one of the two builders who were on the premises at the time, she called out to them to see what they wanted; no one answered. She promptly made her way along the corridor and had a look around only to find no one about, so she went down a level. She called out again and still no one answered. Upon reaching the ground floor she found the two builders working hard, and when asked why they were in that area upstairs, and what they wanted, they told Irene that they had not been on the upper levels of the building at that time and as Irene could clearly see, they were immersed in their graft. As Paddy was out, Irene can only assume that she heard one of the Shakespeare's ghosts as it made its way through one of the inn's upper levels.

The actual bar is not without a spectre too as one of their barmen had quite a nerve-racking experience one day. Cleaning up the pint pots and ashtrays he suddenly became aware of a figure out of the corner of his eye. Thinking nothing of it he continued with his work until he realised that he should have been the only person on the premises at the time. He quickly looked back up to see a black shape – this time in full vision – amble around a corner and disappear. He gave chase and found that when he turned the corner no one was there. After searching the entire premises and finding no one, he realised that he was still in the building alone. No one knows who these phantoms are and efforts to find out have proved fruitless.

A team of paranormal investigators spent the night there a few years ago and came up with a girl who reputedly hanged herself on the premises. This information, I presume, was brought forward by the team psychic, but unfortunately no records of a hanging in this area can be found. The 'investigators' also promised the landlord a full report of their findings – which he is still waiting for to this day!

I guess the identities of the alleged ghosts of the Shakespeare Tavern will have to wait for the time being, as the landlord is now quite reluctant to allow research teams in to investigate due to the actions, or lack of actions in this case, of certain members of our ghost-hunting fraternity.

The Dun Cow

The Dun Cow is a delightful little public house situated at 37 Old Elvet and is more or less opposite the old Durham Jail and courthouse. During my research for this book I ventured into Durham City on many occasions, and, on one of those occasions, whilst exploring the old Elvet area I came across this quaint pub. As far as records show the pub can be dated back to 1837, but it is believed that the building was in fact a 'trading pub' prior to that date; no one knows exactly when the building was first used as an inn.

The pub is not hard to miss as its black and white, brick and wood Tudor style exterior sticks out like a sore thumb as it nestles between the not-so-old looking stone buildings that are either Georgian or Victorian. As I walked up Old Elvet towards the inn I noticed that it was named the Dun Cow. As I had recently finished writing up the introduction for this book (which mentions the legend of the Dun Cow), it inspired me to venture inside and enquire about any potential ghosts that the pub may have had, and my gut instinct paid off.

As I walked in through the doorway I ambled into an area that looked like a thin alley with a roof covering it over. The pub's main entrance was to my immediate right and halfway down the alley was the pub's lounge entrance. Further still were the ladies' and gents' loos and a small courtyard. It was at the lounge door that I chose to enter the pub. When I went in through the door, I came across a lady behind the bar who was busy serving food. I subsequently found out that this lady was the landlord's wife, Audrey.

The Dun Cow pub at 37 Old Elvet is a wonderful old inn that is haunted by a spectral woman. She was seen on one occasion sitting in the corner of the bar by two women at the same time.

The Dun Cow's owner, Mike Leonard.

'Hello, and what can I do for you love?' she said.

I stated my business, told her why I was in Durham and then asked her if the pub was reputed to be haunted. She told me that she had not seen any ghosts, but admitted that there was a resident spectre that she and her husband had christened 'Mary'. She went on to tell me that if I wanted to know the details of what had been going on in the pub, I should speak to her husband as he had 'experienced paranormal phenomena.' At this point she opened the door at the bottom of the stairs and yelled up for her husband, explaining that 'there was a gentleman there to talk to him about the ghost.'

The landlord came downstairs and introduced himself to me as Mike Leonard, asking if I would like to take a seat. He went on to tell me that he had been the landlord at this pub on two occasions (from 2000-2004 and then from 2006-present) and in that time had experienced quite a lot of strange occurrences – objects seemingly moving about on their own, glasses 'clinking' and 'chinking' behind the bar when no one was there. He also stated that the 'ghost' tampers with the beer pumps in the cellars, finding on many occasions during the busiest times in the pub, the ale simply going off. When checking the pumps for problems, he finds that they have been physically turned off. (What self-respecting pub ghost doesn't play with the pumps in the cellars?)

He also told me about the apparition of a woman in the bar and the strange auditory phenomena that are regularly heard in his flat (above the main bar) while he and his wife are working. Apparently, there is a passageway in his flat that runs parallel to the downstairs serving bar, and it is in this passageway where both he and his wife have heard the thumping and clumping of footfalls as they seem to make their way from one end of the passage to the other. Now he told me that when these footfalls are heard there is never anyone in the flat upstairs – well, not of this world anyway.

As it happens, as we were in the bar chatting, we both heard the sound of footfalls and they were indeed pretty loud. Mike piped up, 'You hear those? It's just like that…thump, thump, thump…All the way along only when no one is up there.' On this occasion it turned out to be his wife popping upstairs to tend to an errand, but at least it illustrated to me just how loud and definite the real phantom footfalls are. In regards to the ghost woman, well…she, to Mike's

The Dun Cow inn sign.

The corner seating area in the bar where the unidentified ghost of a woman was observed by two witnesses at the same time.

knowledge, has been seen on one occasion in the pub, but the interesting thing about this sighting is that two members of staff saw her at the same time.

Former barmaids, Janet White and Heather Cavanagh, were preparing the pub for opening back in early 2006 when they saw the woman sitting in the corner of the bar. Both were stunned as she was not there moments ago; they looked at each other and then looked back to find the woman had completely vanished. She simply could not have ventured out of the only door into the bar for two reasons: she would not have had the time to get up and leave in the time it took both Janet and Heather to look back at her, and the door to the pub was still locked as the pub was not open yet.

As the sighting took place so quickly the girls failed to identify what the ghost was wearing so it is quite hard to establish what period of time she may have belonged to. All we know is that the phantom woman is said to sit in the corner of the bar where she stares solemnly into space before disappearing as quickly as she is noticed. No one has been able to identify this spectral woman and so – as mentioned – they have nicknamed her Mary.

The last word I will leave to the landlord Mike, who says, 'A friendly old woman by all accounts that does no harm whatsoever, she tinkers with the fixtures and fittings, the glasses etc, and we don't mind her one little bit.'

The Fighting Cocks

Standing at the foot of Crossgate where North Road meets Framwellgate Bridge, is the Fighting Cocks pub. This traditional drinking den is situated at the foot of a steep incline that leads visitors to Durham to places such as St Margaret's Church and the old cobbled lane that is known as South Street where, incidentally, the old rectory (site of the outraged wraith) stands at the top of the hill.

The Fighting Cocks is a wonderful boozer that is over 300 years old and sells a whole range of top class lagers, beers and wines. Of course the pub is home to some spirits too, and not just Jack Daniels.

It is owned and run by Paul and Diane Martin who, I was told, have been there a very long time. Diane, it seems, worked there for the first fifteen years and then bought the pub, owning it ever since. She has been in residence at the inn now for thirty years!

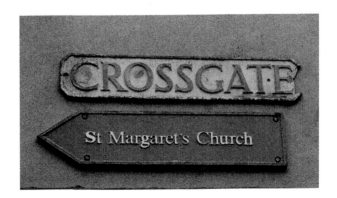

Crossgate and St Margaret's Church.

During my excursions to Durham I couldn't help but be drawn to this pub every time I walked past it. It was as though it was crying out for me to come in and investigate, yet each time I made my way past I chose not to venture inside – I don't know why – I just had the impression that it was 'probably not haunted'. One Sunday morning I arrived in Durham to take some photographs for this book and my route, as it did quite often, took me past this pub. Again, the alehouse caught my eye but this time I decided to act upon my instinct. It was 9.30 a.m. when I pushed the door open to see if I could speak to anyone inside the premises.

As I approached the bar a lady with a warm smile and cheery nature greeted me. I asked her, if by chance, the pub had a resident ghost, and was enthusiastically told that it had not one, but two. I then informed her that I was researching the book and would love to hear the stories of the resident ghosts. The lady was the pub's bar supervisor who, when I asked her name, said she preferred not to say. What she did go on to say, however, was that one of the ghosts of the pub is called Esmeralda. I asked if this was her real name and was informed that Esmeralda was simply a nickname the pub owners and staff had given her. Esmeralda, it seems, made her presence felt quite a lot to the folk in the pub, but not recently.

I asked what type of phenomena was reported there. The bar supervisor went on to say that an abundance of 'odd activity' had been experienced in the main bar area, with glasses being moved around and tinkered with when no one was near them. She also said that the metal trays (used to carry beers on) would be hurled around the bar with cavalier abandon. Ashtrays, when smoking was allowed inside, would also be thrown around with force. I was even told that full pints of ale would fly off the bar before the punter could even pay for them. On one of these occasions it occurred in full view of the bar supervisor and the customer. 'People being touched and prodded in the back are commonplace too,' she said.

I was also informed about the strange noises and thunderous bangs that had been heard by the bar supervisor and other staff when in the bar after it had closed. These noises give the staff such a fright when they occur and they are all at a loss to explain them. I must admit that the sudden displacement of objects, and glasses and trays being thrown around, along with unexplained banging noises, makes me think the haunting could be poltergeist related. The reported phenomenon certainly fits their repertoire.

The Fighting Cocks pub at the foot of Crossgate – haunted by a ghost the staff have nicknamed 'Esmeralda'.

Esmeralda, it seems, prefers to interfere with things and move things around, as opposed to showing herself, although she does put in an appearance from time to time. She is not seen in the bar, but on occasions shows herself down in the cellar and the underground tunnel that is said to lead to another cellar in premises close by. The other ghost is seen a little more often. He is also an unknown shade who has been seen by many as he walks into the gents' loos. On one occasion, a customer noticed the man, who was wearing a long black garment described to me as a cloak, as he went into the toilet. As the customer was also in need of paying a visit, he followed him in. Imagine his surprise when he discovered that he was the only person in the little boys' room at that time. The cubicle doors were all open and there was nowhere for this cloaked individual to go.

At this point the bar supervisor said that was just about all she could tell me but if I was to ring back some time, the owners of the pub could verify and maybe elaborate on what she had told me. I agreed that this is what I would do so I said my thanks and my goodbyes and left the pub. A week later I rang the pub owner, Paul. Paul seemed to be a down-to-earth and no nonsense type of fellow and was quite sceptical in nature, even though he admitted to me that he had seen ashtrays 'exploding and shattering while they were resting on the bar.' He also mentioned that his fridge door shattered, but maintained that there must have been a rational explanation…maybe there was, we just don't know what it is yet.

The cause of the strange phenomena that occurs in this pub from time to time doesn't really matter; the fact is things do happen. One day, possibly when we are all dead and gone, the answers to what we are looking for will reveal themselves in some way, but in the meanwhile if you fancy a good pint and some top class food, I suggest you make a beeline for the Fighting Cocks, for it is one of the finest pubs in the area…oh, and you may just catch a glimpse of their ghosts too.

The Coach and Eight Pub

Let me reiterate something that was said to me in regards to Esmeralda, who allegedly haunts the Fighting Cocks pub. She 'shows herself down in the cellar and the underground tunnel that is said to lead to another cellar in premises close by.' The premises, my dear reader is…yes, you've guessed it, the Coach and Eight pub.

The Coach and Eight pub. Not a pub anymore, however, as it closed down a while ago. The building now stands empty so access was unattainable at the time of writing.

The Coach and Eight is, well, not actually a pub any more and at the time of writing stands empty and disused. This former drinking den was a riverside inn that is situated on / under Framwellgate Bridge and could be accessed by means of a stone flight of stairs which lead down from Framwellgate Bridge. Had I not visited the Fighting Cocks I would never have known that this former pub was haunted. Of course, with the inn now being disused I couldn't actually get in to enquire about the ghost, but I didn't really need to. You see, the bar supervisor at the Fighting Cocks told me all about it.

It turns out that the same ghost that haunts the cellar in the Fighting Cocks is thought to be the ghost that haunts the Coach and Eight. The cellars (as previously mentioned) are apparently joined up by a tunnel that leads from one pub to the other and a short while ago, when the pub was open, the landlord reported a one-off strange occurrence. One day, not long after a new delivery of beer barrels, he ventured in to the cellar to tend to one of his many duties. All was well and he carried out his task with no difficulty. After leaving the cellar for a minute or so he remembered something that he should have done, so made his way back to the cellar. Upon entering the cellar he found – much to his shock – that nine of his new (and full) beer barrels had been stacked up in a neat pyramid. No one could have stacked the barrels up in this way because they were far too heavy. Since the landlord was apparently on his own, only away from the cellar for a minute or two since his last visit, and never actually heard the 'clang' or 'din' that a beer barrel would make when being moved around on a stone floor, we can only assume that it was a result of a playful ghost – and a bloody strong one at that.

The Garden House Hotel

The Garden House Hotel is a very short walk away from Durham City Centre and stands on North Road, which is the old travellers' road that ran from Edinburgh to London. The inn is a well-known Durham landmark, and is as much of a focal point in the area as the neighbouring church. It is a traditional olde world style public house that was built around the early 1700s and was formerly known as the 'Woodman Inn'. This fine drinking hole became known as the Garden House Hotel in the latter part of the nineteenth century and boasts grand old original fireplaces and magnificent oak beams – one of my favourite characteristics in pubs. This beautifully run family pub and B&B has six *en suite* bedrooms on the upper level of the premises, adding much character and charm to the pub. Selling fine wines, real ales, good lagers and traditional style pub grub, the Garden House Hotel really is as good as it gets. The fact that it is reputed to house a ghost or two makes the inn well worth visiting and is, of course, why it features within these pages.

In March 2009 the Ghosts and Hauntings Overnight Surveillance Team arrived at the pub to carry out an overnight investigation (results of which are not yet published). Fellow investigator Fiona Vipond chatted to the publican Paul Mash, and ascertained a little information regarding the ghosts that are thought to reside there. Paul said:

There have been experiences with all the staff that have been here before. Different things have gone on with various staff members noticing different things in certain areas of the pub. There are guest rooms upstairs and untoward things have allegedly occurred in there

The Garden House Hotel at the top of North Road.

with one particular cleaner woman having an experience she won't tell us about. Whatever happened in room 3 not so long ago frightened her to the extent that she is now very dubious about going in there to clean the room. She has said, however, that funny things do go on in that room and has mentioned to me that once she saw something move onto the bed while she was in there. On another occasion she ventured into the room to clean it, and saw an indentation on one of the beds as though someone was actually sitting on it although no one could be seen. Personally, though, I feel the place has nice warmth to it and the alleged ghosts do not worry me in the least.

An artist's impression of the indentation on a bed that was allegedly made by a ghost, and seen by one of the hotel staff while cleaning the room. (Illustration by Julie Olley)

The door in this picture was the old entrance to the Garden House Hotel and it was in this area that the author and Ralph Keeton heard and recorded a ghostly cough or sigh during their investigations here.

After Fiona had chatted with Paul, I decided to see if I could glean any more information from him in regards to the pub's ghosts. He told me that the ghost of a young girl had been seen in the bar area wearing old-fashioned clothing, but when pressed for more information he told me that was all he knew. I asked him if he had seen her and he replied that he had not. He did mention that the resident Chef, Steve Clough, for some reason did not like the original entrance to the bar and felt that there was indeed something – although he could not say what – residing down in that area. Granted, not scientific or hard objective evidence of a haunting, but it was all we had to go on and it seemed interesting enough.

So, is the pub haunted? Well, its seems there have been a few occasions where the staff and owners have become convinced that it is, and given its history and its age it is very likely to house a spectre or two from bygone days. Our investigation there proved mediocre, with one or two strange occurrences being witnessed. It's hard to say with any certainty whether the pub is or isn't haunted until further documented *bona fide* reports of ghost sightings come in, or further tests are carried out.

three

INVESTIGATIONS AND OVERNIGHT CASE STUDIES

Witton Castle

Where better to begin our overnight investigation section of 'Haunted Durham' than at Witton Castle in Bishop Auckland, County Durham. Strictly speaking, Witton Castle is not actually within the geographical remit of this book but due to its association with Durham City I feel it warrants inclusion in this volume. That, combined with the fact that it is one of Durham's finest fortified bastions with an amazing history, and has a number of alleged ghosts.

Witton Castle and Park is home to one of the finest caravan and camping sites that County Durham has, and proves to be a very popular haunt for tourists from all over the North-East and beyond. Situated in the heart of beautiful Durham countryside, Witton Castle really is a great base for holidaymakers who wish to explore neighbouring areas such as Northumbria, near Durham City, or one of the other places of interest such as the many wonderful stately homes and historic buildings County Durham has to offer. Amidst 330 acres of beautiful landscape scenery at the foot of the Pennines, this fourteenth-century castle forms the centrepiece of the park and the surrounding countryside. It is home to an abundance of varied wildlife, is in an ideal setting for contemplation and solitude, and provides a peaceful haven for visitors to Witton Castle.

For those who like life a bit more lively, the castle has an entertainment bar and function room that provides revellers with a fine selection of ales, spirits and wines along with 'entertainment nights' such as discos and even bingo for the more mature holidaymaker. Take-away cafés, gift shops, games rooms and a grocery store are also available to the holidaymaker in the summer season. Stables that offer horse and pony rides, child-safe play parks with Lazer Quest and

The magnificent frontage of Witton Castle. (Courtesy of Andrew Local)

The impressive tall walls of Witton Castle. (Courtesy of Andrew Local)

Paintball are also all available for the younger generation, making Witton Castle and Park one of the most well-equipped caravan parks in the whole of County Durham. Today the castle is owned and run by Karen Hague who ensures that during your stay you are looked after well and all your needs are catered for.

Witton castle is almost unique in some respects, because unlike most of the other historic castles in the North of England, Witton has never been the ancestral home for any one family for very long. The family that has occupied the castle the longest in its varied history is the Eure family who acquired the lands sometime in the early fourteenth century. The Eure family was a warring family, and due to their part in fighting against the Scots, they were greatly rewarded by King Edward I. In the early fourteenth century, Ralph Eure began to build Witton Castle upon the lands they had recently acquired, but due to the lack of planning permission from the relevant authorities, he landed himself in deep trouble. Before long, and due to his status, he was given a pardon along with the necessary licence to carry on and subsequently build his castle. Parts of Witton Castle today actually date from that time.

The Eure family continued their warring at every opportunity and eventually Ralph Eure was knighted by the king and became Sir Ralph Eure. Unfortunately, his knighthood was short lived as during the Battle of Towton in 1461, he was killed. The Battle of Towton was a vital battle in the War of the Roses in which the white rose Lancastrian cause was defeated and Edward of York became Edward IV.

The Great Hall. (Courtesy of Andrew Local)

Sir Ralph's son, William Eure, married into the great Northumbrian family, the Percys, whose magnificent castle in Alnwick is still in their tenure. Under King Henry VIII, William Eure continued his fight against the Scots and was subsequently made captain of Berwick-upon-Tweed, and its castle. At the outbreak of the Civil War, the owner of Witton Castle was William, 6th Lord Eure, who was a Cavalier Colonel that fell at the regiment of horse at Marston Moor in 1644 – the battle that marked the turning point in the Civil War against the Royalists and ushered in eleven years of inhospitable Cromwellian repression. Since William bore no sons, Witton Castle was succeeded by a distant cousin, the 7th Baron, who in turn sold the castle to a Royalist called Sir William D'Arcy.

The Eure ownership was now over and a new family were set to become the lords of the manner. Lord D'Arcy held the castle for the king for a time and during this period the castle was besieged by rebels who were under Sir Arthur Hazlerigg, the Governor of West Auckland. Although the castle was captured it suffered very little damage, and after the war Lord D'Arcy was forced to literally pay for his errors in the form of a fine. Witton was rather fortunate in regards to the many other sieges that were taking place due to its position being well off the main southern route. Armies that were crossing from east to west preferred to use the more southerly route near Stainmore Pass. It is thought, however, that the Parliamentarians may have occupied the castle in 1648 and in 1651 when the Anglo-Scots Royalist armies were passing through Cumbria.

Sir William D'Arcy had one brother, James D'Arcy, of Sedbury Park near Richmond in Yorkshire and it was his son, Lord D'Arcy of Navan who inherited the castle. He had no use for the castle and so, in 1689, he began to dismantle it to enlarge and improve his own home in Sedbury. At the beginning of the eighteenth century Witton Castle was rebuilt and in 1743 it changed hands again to yet another D'Arcy. He also preferred to live at Sedbury so he sold the castle on to one William Cuthbert, who was a barrister and recorder of Newcastle. After William's son John died, the castle went to another family by marriage. John's sister, Philadelphia, married a friend of her brother's called Ralph Hopper and it was their son (also called John) who went on to inherit the castle.

On 27 December 1796 disaster struck the castle in the form of a great fire that gutted the entire building. The interior was completely destroyed and only the shell of the castle remained. No one was hurt during the outbreak but everything inside the castle was lost forever. John Hopper died in 1812 when he fell down a flight of stairs at Witton Castle, with the castle subsequently going to the authorities. It wasn't until four years later in 1816 when the castle was put up for sale, and on 10 October of that year (1816) the burned-out shell of the fortress was purchased by William Chaytor for the grand sum of £78,000.

William Chaytor was a Member of Parliament and therefore a man of considerable wealth. He was able to completely restore and refurbish Witton Castle to its former glory and made it his family seat for some considerable time. In 1831 he was created a baronet, and after the Reform Act of 1833 he was elected to Parliament for the city of Sunderland. After almost twenty-five years at Witton Castle he sold it on to Donald MacLean in 1839 for a tidy sum of £100,000. MacLean, who was a fraudster that actually conned William Chaytor out of his money, then held a feasting and drinking party that lasted three days and nights at Witton before eventually fleeing abroad owing money to just about everyone. The castle came back to the Chaytor family while the whole sorry mess was sorted out.

Bringing things up to date, in 1963 Witton Castle was bought by the Viscount of Lambton who was the son of the late 5th Earl of Durham. With the purchase of Witton by Lord Lambton the castle once more came into the hands of a Eure family member as Frances Eure was the wife of Robert Lambton, and was granddaughter of the 1st Lord Eure who was descended from the ancient Eure family that once owned the castle. Nowadays the castle is owned by Karen Hague and family. Her son, Adam Hague, was kind enough to provide me with the aforementioned information in regards to the castle's history.

Of course, Witton Castle is not without its ghosts. With castles like this one, there is usually an abundance of resident spectres that aimlessly walk the corridors, stalk the battlements and generally linger around forever in search of peace, for whatever reason, and Witton is no different. On the night of 25 April 2009 the Ghosts and Hauntings, Overnight Surveillance Team conducted an investigation there in the hope of discovering and documenting some paranormal phenomena. While chatting, I asked the owners' son Adam if he had personally witnessed any of the alleged ghosts that are said to reside there and he told me that he had not. Adam spends little time at the castle and informed me that I should speak to the castle's secretary, Meg Armstrong, who knew a lot more in regards to the paranormal occurrences that have been witnessed there.

The downstairs bar. From the adjoining room the author heard unexplained footfalls and movement when the actual room in question was empty. (Courtesy of Andrew Local)

Upon chatting with Meg, I discovered a whole range of ghosts that are said to haunt the castle. Strangely enough the ghosts don't reside in the usual parts of the castle, such as the Great Hall or the Tapestry room, but rather the private living quarters of some of the staff and the basement bar where our base room was for the night. In regards to alleged ghosts in the downstairs bar, near to the beer cellar, she went on to say:

Well, I have been here over ten years now and people that I have worked with, including the present bar manager, really don't like to come to this area on their own. On one occasion while the bar manager was down in the bar, he felt an awful feeling that he was not alone. Not long after, a Lemonade bottle that was behind the actual bar was thrown over his shoulder from behind him, which smashed on the floor. The ladies' toilets, which are housed in this area, are haunted too. Another team of investigators that spent the night here reported seeing a peculiar black mist as it drifted out from one of the cubicles and across the room where it disappeared through the wall. They also claimed that a mother and child were walled up behind one of the walls in this area, which is the cause of a ghost boy that has been seen in this area. The ghost boy tale holds some validity, as there is indeed a ghost of a young lad that has been seen by one of our visitor's children as she was in the loos. After spending twenty minutes in there, the mother of this young child obviously became a little worried and began to look for her. She eventually found her in these loos. When her mother asked where she had been all this time, the young girl replied by saying that she had been talking to a strangely dressed small boy that lives in the castle. There is no small boy living at the castle.

I asked Meg about any other ghosts that were said to reside in other parts of the castle. She told me:

They say someone died on the main stairwell leading up into the castle and his ghost is said to have been seen in this area. And outside near the main entrance there has been horses and a carriage heard as it thunders around the oval shaped drive. There are a few people that have heard that, with the funny thing being that there is actually nothing to see. Only the noises of the coach and horses are heard as it pulls up to the entrance.

It is interesting to note that the ghost of a man has been seen on the stairs in the castle, and I may actually have a name to go with this apparition. I am probably not the first to make this connection, and those who are versed in the castle's history should piece it together. Mentioned earlier in this chapter are details of one John Hopper who fell down a flight of stairs at Witton Castle and died – perhaps the ghost that has been observed on the main stairwell is his? Until we can get descriptions of both the apparition, and of course John Hopper, I guess we can't be sure.

It seemed that the area where we were based for the investigation was the main area for the alleged hauntings and although our team were granted permission to 'access all areas,' our investigation would be primarily in these parts. Some of the private living quarters for the staff were also 'open for investigation' as they were allegedly haunted too, but nothing much of a paranormal nature occurred during these vigils.

Two other ghosts were said to haunt the castle, one being a macabre and sinister looking man who has been seen quite often in the flat that the owners' son Adam uses when he stays over at the castle, and the other being a large horse that has been seen and heard on the castle stairs inside the main entrance; very peculiar.

It was now time to begin our investigations so we split up into our respective groups. A number of the castle staff joined us for the investigation, including Adam Hague, who was placed in my care for the evening. It must be stressed that prior to the investigation beginning, and before I carried out my interviews with Adam and Meg, I experienced what I believe to be paranormal activity in the main bar area downstairs. I had been outside getting some air and upon my return to the base room I found it was completely empty. I grabbed my camera in order to take a few photographs of the bar area and the adjoining room and ventured through to the back of the other room to take my pictures.

As I turned and looked towards the door area I distinctly heard the sound of someone moving around in the area where all our bags were. Footfalls were heard, along with creaking and movement upon the bar room floor. I also heard the rustling of something which I couldn't identify. I raised my camera to take my picture and found that my batteries, which had been recharging all day, were drained of all their power and so I was unable to take my picture. I could still hear the movement coming from the other room so I went through to see if one of the team, or one of the guests, had returned. To my utter surprise, I walked in to find the noises ceased abruptly and found no one at all in there. I really thought that someone had returned, not thinking for one second it was (or could have been) one of the castle's ghosts.

Another view of Witton's incredible castle. (Courtesy of Andrew Local)

In the distance I heard some voices so I traced them to the beer cellar whereupon I asked everyone in there, 'has anyone been messing about in the base room?' I was told that no one had been in that room as they were all too busy chatting at the back of the cellar. So, it remains a mystery as to what, or whom it was that I heard moving around.

We began the investigation with a reading from Ralph Keeton who picked up and sensed some incredible things in regards to the castle, its history and it ghosts. During the reading he was given the name Ralph, but couldn't decide if it was someone calling his name, or a spirit telling him his name was Ralph. As we know, in the early fourteenth century Ralph Eure began to build Witton Castle and is known for his connection to the property. Ralph Keeton told us all about the horse that has been heard on the stairwell (not common knowledge) and mentioned that a fire had ripped through the building in days gone by…he was correct. It must also be stressed that Ralph Keeton had no idea where he was investigating that night and was brought to the venue by Andrew Local who had met Ralph earlier at a designated meeting point. This was so the medium could not do any research prior to his arrival.

Throughout the course of the investigation we tried many experiments including our trigger objects, where something is drawn around and left in the hope that spiritual interaction is achieved with it. Many Electronic Voice Recordings (EVPs) were carried out, along with all our usual investigation practices, with very little happening in the way of paranormal phenomena. We investigated the castle from top to bottom and even spent some time outside on the oval drive in the hope we might hear the ghostly carriage pulling in – we did not. CCTV that was set up recorded nothing of any interest, and the other lock off video cameras also proved fruitless. There were, however, a number of incidences that were reported by the team during their vigils. Mark Winter heard what he described as a 'long drawn-out sigh' coming from the empty part of the upstairs bar area, and Drew Bartley claimed to have had his arm violently tugged at while investigating the upper levels of the castle.

Although these incidences were reported (along with my encounter in the main bar), GHOST consider this to have been a rather quiet investigation. When you have seen objects being hurled around, doors slamming closed, trigger objects being thrown about or even stolen from under your nose by 'ghosts', and investigators being physically assaulted by invisible entities (Drew Bartley, Thurcroft Institute in Rotherham), investigations such as Witton Castle are deemed rather tame – taking nothing away from Witton Castle, of course, as it is a truly magnificent place to spend the night investigating. Fiona Vipond hit the nail on the head when she said, 'You see, just because the venue is a large spooky castle, people think that it is bound to be alive with paranormal activity…it just goes to show, doesn't it?'

We did experience a little odd phenomena and one day we hope to return to re-investigate the castle and its grounds.

The City Hotel

Our next investigation takes us to an olde world drinking establishment in central Durham. Located on 'New Elvet', which is just around the corner from the infamous haunted inn Jimmy Allen's, the City Hotel is a 500-year-old former manor house that oozes charm, character, and a warm welcome.

The City Hotel on New Elvet.

On a dark and cold January night we arrived there to carry out a series of scientific tests and experiments. Not much is known about the City Hotel regarding its history and whether or not it does have ghosts and so this investigation was simply diagnostic. We arrived in Durham at about 10.30 p.m. and made our way to the hotel where the (then) owner Paul Wray met us. We made ourselves comfortable and waited for Ralph Keeton (our medium) and guest Nikki Austwicke to arrive, which they did at about 11 p.m. We chatted for about an hour whilst waiting for the pub to empty and, when it did, we set about our usual pre-investigation tasks. The baselines were carried out first followed by a reading from our medium.

For our investigation we were allowed access into six of the hotel rooms, the 200-year-old grand staircase and the main bar downstairs. Throughout the baseline tests we determined that no areas showed anomalous readings in regards to the EMF sweeps, and the average temperature of the rooms was 18-19°C. A few windows were noted to have a slight draught coming from outside and one or two rooms had some very squeaky floorboards, so care was taken not to misinterpret any possible phenomena that really would have had a natural cause. The bar showed a temperature reading of 24°C, but not less than twenty minutes before this the room was full of revellers, so I think body heat would account for this.

Medium Ralph Keeton gets to work on what turned out to be a very interesting investigation.

We began the reading of the City Hotel at about 1 a.m. and it was filmed and recorded for documentation purposes. Our first area for investigation was the front of the bar and this is what Ralph told us:

> In this area I am standing in now there is a young girl. She is about thirteen/fourteen years old and has very long hair, very, very long hair indeed. She would have been reported, if anyone had seen her as what is called a white ghost! While chatting to you guys she literally floated in here and it is this area in which she wanders. Rather than make the area go cold, this girl does the opposite and makes people feel rather hot and sweaty – it's a bit like a hot spot rather than a cold spot. I think one or two may have seen her and she is going to come through tonight. She either lived here or has been associated with this building somehow as she knows it quite well and we may see a flash of white light in this area as this is how she will show herself to us.

We moved down the bar, stood in the area where the pool table was, and continued with the reading when Ralph picked up on the fact that the place was in actual fact two buildings rather than one. Paul, the owner, confirmed that this was true. Ralph then asked if a chimney, or an open fire, had being taken out of this area and, that too, was confirmed by the owner. Ralph continued:

This is going to sound pretty obvious but you are going to have movement around this bar area and wisps of smoke and mist have occurred here. You also have a door that needs to be slammed closed at times.

This too was confirmed as correct as Paul verified that the fire exit door sticks and has to be closed with force.

'Is there a recurring problem in the ladies' loos?' Ralph asked.

'No,' came the reply.

At this point Paul and his colleagues began to smile and laugh.

'So why are you laughing?' I asked them.

'Because we have the problem in the gents' loos!' They said.

'You see, I am getting the ladies'…with me it's the ladies' loos. I am going to go down there, I need to see what I feel when I go down there,' Ralph said.

We walked to the bottom of the corridor and immediately Ralph turned to the wall on the left-hand side and said, 'I want to go that way.'

'You can't, we don't know what is in there, but we do know it used to be part of this building,' came the reply.

Ralph said:

Yes, I can feel it. I feel like I want to walk that way. I also feel sick down here because I have the feeling that anyone coming down this way may indeed feel sick and that is due to the presence that is down here. He is a prankster and likes to joke around by making people feel ill at ease and it is this guy that blocks up the loos, he is a total joker and we are going to have some fun down here later on.

'It's quite interesting that you said the word "he,"' Nikki said.

'Did I?' said Ralph. 'That is interesting, I must be subconsciously picking up that this is a male then.'

We then ventured back into the main bar and Ralph picked up on a spirit presence that had just come to him. It transpired that this was a reading from a spirit who turned out to be highly significant to the pub, the owners, the bar staff and locals, so due to obvious and personal reasons, I will not elaborate on what was picked up on and more importantly, who came through to Ralph. What I will say is that this reading was almost perfect in every way and things were sensed that no one could have known except the pub owners and the barman. The look on the barman's face after the reading said it all.

Ralph then picked up on the dates 1840-1842 and told us that a hangman or executioner once stayed or lived on these premises. Then he talked about three creaky steps on an upper level and asked if there were any. He felt that someone walks on these stairs, and when they tread on these three particular stairs, people become aware of their presence. He then asked to go upstairs to continue his reading. When we reached the 200-year-old stairwell, almost immediately he decided everything was all wrong.

'I am all disjointed, I don't feel right here. The layout, the walls are all in the wrong place and I feel the grand staircase should go down where the floor is now situated and again I just want to go this way' (pointing to the wall).

Again Paul, the owner, confirmed that this was correct and there were indeed more stairs that led down from where we were standing. There was also another area of building, which wasn't there now. This is where Ralph had wanted to go.

'Beeston or Beaston,' he then said, 'Who is Beeston?'

Ralph then told us that we would get some paranormal activity down the corridor which led to rooms 4-6, so, obviously, we all had a walk down. He subsequently told us of a large, slightly deaf, woman who was very domineering and bossy. He also told us that the level of the floor was not at its original height and said it should be far higher up. Then he said there was a weird ghostly smell connected to this area and at that point I felt a cold draught or breeze blow right across my face. Drew Bartley felt another cold draught while sitting in room 4. Were things starting to warm up?

This was where the reading started to become rather odd for the author in more ways than one. Ralph explained that this domineering woman had an affinity for me and was drawn forwards when she heard my voice. He said there was a Scottish connection with her and she attached herself to me when I came to this area. I then felt dizzy and disorientated, finding it hard to focus, but said nothing...just yet. I thought it might have just been me feeling odd, yet I also thought maybe it was the spirit woman making me feel this way. Ralph then said, to my utter astonishment, that people would often feel disorientated and dizzy while up in this area!

'I've got swords,' he said, 'Two swords crossed over.'

I began to think, for some strange reason, that Ralph was starting to read me because I own two swords: a wooden one called a bokken, and a steel samurai sword from Japan. I told him about my swords.

'You have two swords?' he asked, surprised.

'Do you have problems with your jaw or your tooth or some problem inside your mouth at the minute?'

'I do indeed,' and I went on to tell him what I had been experiencing lately.

'Right, we are going somewhere with this. The woman we have with us here recognises these similarities between you and herself and that is why she likes you,' Ralph said.

'So this hand,' he continued, 'I am talking about this finger, which is your left hand, and the middle finger is sore. A joint or knuckle that has been broken or dislocated and is now in pain.'

I told him that this very knuckle was broken during some martial arts training a few years ago. It all seemed surreal as what he was saying tied in with lots of different little aspects of my life.

'So why has she latched onto Darren?' Drew said.

After a few seconds of deep thought and concentration Ralph said, 'It's his voice; she is recognising Darren's voice. The more you speak the more she will come forward as she finds you very interesting,' he said. 'If you do a vigil up here later on and you ask for phenomena you will get it, that I promise.'

At this point I became very dizzy again and nearly lost my balance. I felt unwell with it and this time I mentioned it to everyone.

'This is what I felt too,' Ralph said. 'This lady has made a very strong connection with you, the more you speak the more she comes forwards towards you.'

At this point in the proceedings I decided to leave the area because I could barely string a sentence together through being disorientated and dizzy, combined with feeling quite

The 200-year-old wooden stairwell inside the City Hotel.

apprehensive and unnerved. We left the area for the time being, and ended Ralph's reading. Little did I know that this was the start of something incredible.

After a short break we decided it was time to split into groups and investigate the building to see if we could experience and document any paranormal phenomena. Drew, Jason (a guest) and myself went back to rooms 4-6 to see if we would get any activity, while Lee, Fiona and Jonathon (another guest) went to rooms 2 and 3 and Ralph, Nikki and Andy (another guest) went along the corridor next to the toilets. Since time was getting on we designated ourselves thirty minutes in each location before coming back down for a short break.

We arrived back upstairs and more or less immediately I began to feel disorientated and dizzy again, so I called out to this alleged spirit lady in the hope that she would give us a real sign. After a while nothing was happening so I tried again. It was then that Drew swept me with his EMF meter and we ascertained a reading of 2 MG. We then went into room 4 and sat down for a while. I called out again and asked for signs and it was at this point 2.49 a.m. Both Drew and I clearly heard someone whistling from down the corridor. Now we know for a fact that no one was down there at the time, so who whistled we could not say…yet!

The rest of this vigil was quite interesting as we heard a loud bang or a series of bangs, which sounded like a rumbling noise, which we were at a loss to explain. Our guest, Jason, described it as furniture being dragged across the floor. It seems Ralph's prediction for phenomena in this area due to my being there was proved correct! We then ventured into room 6 along the corridor and held a séance during which one or two light anomalies were caught on night vision video camera. After the vigil had finished we went downstairs for a short break. After this break, we returned to the location upstairs, only this time we decided to bring Ralph to see if he could continue his reading of the area…and maybe me.

At 3.30 a.m. Ralph told us that the spirit lady was only coming forward tonight because I was present. He told us that this was her area and where she will stay. In other words, she will not be coming home with me after the investigation. (Which, in all honesty, I was rather pleased to hear.) At this point in the investigation I was leaning against the wall with my right arm whilst listening to Ralph, when all of a sudden I was pushed from behind at the elbow making me stumble forward a little.

'You were just pushed there,' Ralph said.

'It sure felt like it,' I said.

Then within the space of five minutes the same thing happened again, only this time it felt a little harder. At this precise time a light anomaly was filmed right behind me. I then felt weirdly exhilarated and the feeling of delight overcame me for reasons I could not say. We moved back into room 6 and the reading and the investigation continued:

Now, I am going to tell you what I got when I was talking to the others downstairs, I am getting the impression that this building was used for pirates, now when I say pirates I don't mean the seafaring swashbuckling vagabonds that sail the high seas in search of treasures, no! I mean it was a place for storage of illegal things and I must stress it's not recent. We are going back a good few years here!

At this point, I decided to call out to the atmosphere in the hope that this lady would give us another sign and then I started to see little light anomalies with my naked eye floating about the room. These anomalies were not the usual kind, and when I say that I mean they were not white, or bright lights, but quite the opposite. These little spots of…whatever it was I was seeing…were black in colour! I thought it may have been my eyes playing tricks in the dark, but Ralph assured me it was not.

He then said that the spirit lady who has the affinity with me was standing close by, and seemed to be leaning over me as though she was pressing herself upon me. He then got a sensation of absolute pain and agony coming from her and said this pain goes back to about 1827. He said she was now next to me and touching my head!

'Fish, Fish…she hates fish,' Ralph said, as he began to hold his throat. 'Why is she telling me to tell you that?'

At this point in the reading I went white as a sheet as I was simultaneously overcome with surprise and shock. That very day at work while eating my lunch, which consisted of a scabby portion of chips, a pile of mush those at the work canteen call peas… and a battered fish, I had a very large fishbone stuck and lodged in my throat, and I literally thought I was going to choke to death on it. It was stuck (although I could breathe…just!) for about twenty-five minutes until it became dislodged and swallowed with some dry bread I was told to eat by a woman at a neighbouring table. I subsequently left the rest of my lunch and decided I was going to give fish a wide berth from that point on!

'Well she has literally told me to tell you this, she wanted you to know this.'

He then said to me the strangest thing, 'Why have you cried? Have you been crying?'

Again you could have knocked me down with a feather. Just that morning before I went to work there was an incident at my home involving our (then seven-month-old) daughter Abbey that resulted in my partner Jayne and I shedding a few tears. I will not elaborate on what actually happened but I did indeed cry a little that morning. I hadn't cried or shed tears for a good few years (except the day she was born of course) and I did that day, and for Ralph to pick up on that really did astound me. He said to me,

'I am seeing through your crying eyes.'

I explained what had happened and he went on to say that this woman knew that I had been crying when I came into her domain this evening and wanted me to know that everything would be alright in regards to what happened. Now, writing these words after the event, I am glad to know that Ralph, and the lady in question, was indeed right and my daughter is absolutely fine, as are Jayne and myself. The vigil then came to an end and we re-grouped in the bar downstairs for a break.

That night's investigation is one I will not forget in a hurry and my experiences with the reading I received from Ralph, combined with my ill-at-ease feelings earlier on, really made me think hard about everything and had a very profound effect upon me – but the night was not over yet. We still had one more investigation location to stake out and that was the corridor that led to the toilets. After our final break we headed down the corridor to the toilet area, made ourselves comfortable and started to call out to the atmosphere in the hope of getting some good paranormal activity. It was so dark down there you could not see your hand in front of your face and as I began to attempt spirit communication, we all became aware of what sounded like a man's guttural breath or someone clearing their throat. It was certainly not one of the investigators and it came from directly behind where I was standing, which was with my back facing the gents' toilets, as I was peering round the corner along the corridor.

After a discussion of what, or who, it could have been, we called out again to this spirit man. It is interesting to note that when Ralph was reading this area earlier on he claimed the spirit down there was indeed a man. It looks as though he was correct again. Time went by and nothing else seemed to be happening until we all heard the shuffling of footsteps coming from the opposite end of the corridor. Upon inspection of the area we found nothing untoward and no one was around to account for the shuffling we heard. It seemed this vigil was producing some good results. The trigger object we had placed down the corridor failed to move and the EMF and temperature surveys provided no anomalous readings.

The end of the vigil and investigation quickly came so we tied up our loose ends, finished off the experiments, gathered up the equipment and headed off home for some well-deserved rest. In summary, the investigation was rather good for me personally as I was subjected to what I believe was some very strange phenomena. Along with the reading from Ralph, it certainly made this an investigation to remember. The rest of the group's investigations unfortunately provided me with very little in the way of information as a quiet night was had. There was the occasional knock and bump, a feeling of coldness but nothing that could have been deemed credible and objective paranormal phenomena, as one of the investigators told me. I guess working with a medium most of the night does break the monotony of what may otherwise be a dull and long evening with only few possible phenomena encountered. Having said that, working without a medium can be just as rewarding if one is patient and tenacious. This particular investigation was very satisfying indeed and I look forward to a second investigation at this, one of the oldest and most historic hotels in Durham City Centre.

A Church Hall

Our next investigation and this time we were staking out an old church hall, which is situated within Durham City Centre. It is still used as a church hall and community centre today, and dates back to 1902. It stands on the opposite side of the road from the church whose name it shares (which must remain anonymous due to the nature of this particular building and also at the request of the key holders).

The building in question includes a large hall, a central corridor, two smaller joined congregation rooms and the parish administrative centre, which was established a few years ago. It is here, at this undisclosed location, that tea and coffee are served after the parish communion on Sunday mornings, and it is often used for other public occasions organised by the church and local community. Our visit here was with the sole purpose of yet another diagnostic examination, as no reports whatsoever, as far as we were aware, have come in regarding any ghostly phenomena that may have occurred there.

On the night in question we arrived in Durham for the investigation. The building is quite new in comparison to some of the other venues we have investigated in the past, but nevertheless it is still over 100 years old. A lot can happen in 100 years, so we remained hopeful. When we arrived we set up our base room, which was in the main hall and proceeded to carry out the initial reading of the premises and rooms with the North-East Ghost Research Team and (then) GHOST team psychic Suzanne Hitchinson.

The reading began in the main hall and it was there where she told us about the spirit of a man whom she felt walks the premises. She told us he was nothing to be afraid of as he was a benevolent soul, and was just interested in what we were doing. We moved into the central corridor that runs through the building and she subsequently said that this man had followed us through. At this precise time a moving light anomaly was caught on infrared night vision video camera. She picked nothing else up at this point so we moved into the two back rooms.

In the back rooms it was brought to our attention by Suzanne that a relative of a former priest or vicar had lived in this particular area, as it was once a vicarage. It was after the vicarage was used that the relative occupied this living space. The name Alexander came forward and later she sensed a young woman called Murphy.

'Mmm! An Irish connection,' I said.

Onwards into the back storeroom, which Suzanne said had once been used as kennels. Nothing more came to her at that point so we ventured upstairs into the office and continued

A church hall.

with the reading. In here she told us of a male spirit, an authoritative and strict man, and said he had a different energy to that of the man downstairs.

Now we had a basic idea of what was what, and it was time to carry out our preliminary baseline tests throughout the building. A sweep with the EMF meter in all locations showed no anomalous readings and the average temperature of the building was between 22-24°C. We placed a number of trigger objects down including a crucifix, a flour tray containing a ball and some batteries, and placed down two sets of beam barriers and motion sensors – one on the staircase and one in the central corridor. We were ready to begin the investigations.

We split into two groups with Suzanne McKay and myself in group one, and Lee Stephenson, Drew Bartley, and Fiona Vipond in group two. Whilst group two investigated the back rooms, group one stayed in the main hall. Not a great deal happened with group two, except for one or two light anomalies being caught on camera at 1.18 a.m. and 1.25 a.m. and a cold draught felt at 1.30 a.m. However, in our vigil a strong smell of fish was smelt by both Suzanne and myself, and the rustling of paper was heard emanating from the darkness. Inspection found no rational cause for this smell or the auditory phenomena.

A dictation machine that was left recording in this location while we called out for phenomena left us with no results. But it was at 1.33 a.m. when the first visual phenomenon came. Whilst I was standing at the table writing my notes, Suzanne saw what she describes as a 6ft black shadow move across the back wall. This gave her something of a fright and she thought it might have been me casting an actual shadow. Tests proved it was not. Feelings of pain and stiffness down Suzanne's left side led her to think that someone in the not-too-distant past may have suffered a heart attack or a stroke in this particular area. Between then, and the end of this vigil, nothing much else was reported, so we re-grouped and had a break.

After the break, group one headed off into the back rooms where group two had previously been, and group two headed upstairs to the parish administrative centre. During this location Suzanne decided to try some rod dowsing but the results were not too good. The rods did indeed indicate a presence; however, the information given by the 'source' proved rather disappointing. I wandered off into the adjoining storeroom and left Suzanne sitting on the floor. It was not long before we were treated to some fantastic phenomena, which I caught on my dictation machine and my video camera. You can clearly hear the sound of what we think was a coin hitting a wall, bouncing off the wooden floor and then rolling for a few seconds before hitting the back wall skirting board. It made some considerable noise and it surprised both Suzanne and myself. We spent the rest of this vigil trying to work out what had happened. We could not. What we do know is that we picked up auditory paranormal phenomena.

Group two's vigil proved rather interesting, with light anomalies being recorded on video camera, and a cold, tingling feeling was reported by Drew Bartley on his arm. Not much else happened during this vigil, or so they thought until the EVP machine was played back during the break. What we heard astounded us all beyond belief and would even send shivers down the spine of the most sceptical people.

Recorded on the EVP machine was a series of unexplained voices, which we can all verify are not ours! The first voice I believe to be an Irish lady and she is heard saying 'CAN YOU HELP ME?'

Oddly enough, immediately after this voice you can hear Drew Bartley in the background claiming to have caught a strange light on his video camera and it was then that he went cold.

This woman's voice was not heard at the time! Coincidence? I think not.

The second of these amazing EVP recordings was about ten minutes after the first when Fiona Vipond was calling out for phenomena. In between Fiona talking you can clearly hear the sound of a woman in a gentle and loving voice saying, 'NIGHTIE-NIGHT THEN, THE NIGHT IS OVER.'

I think this voice is the same as the first one as this too sounds Irish. The last EVP to be recorded in this vigil appeared about five minutes after the second voice and fifteen minutes after the first one. It simply said, 'PICK ME UP.'

These sound recordings were taped by Lee Stephenson's EVP machine and what the voices are and where they came from is still a mystery, but many people believe we have recorded the voices of ghosts or earth-bound spirits that are calling out for help, as if trapped between the two worlds. Perhaps we have, but one thing that was certain on the night was that when we heard them for the first time, our blood ran cold! It was a fantastic result.

After an extra long break it was group one's turn to spend some time in the room where the recordings had just been made. In all honesty I was quite apprehensive, as was Suzanne, but nevertheless we ventured up with a positive attitude in the hope that we too would get some results. We slowly crept up the stairs, half expecting to see the ghost woman when we turned the corner to go into the room but alas, this did not happen.

We settled down in the office and proceeded with the investigation. Just on the off-chance, I decided to leave my audio dictation machine running whilst in there and in retrospect I am glad I did, as yet another anomalous voice recording was made. I will talk about this recording soon, but first I must point out that the trigger objects that I had previously placed into my flour tray had been moved. To be more precise, one of the batteries had been pushed over. It must be stressed that we had just looked at the trigger objects when we entered the room and they were just as we had left them. It is possible that the battery just fell over, but this seems highly improbable as they were pushed deep into the flour. It seemed it had been moved while we were in the room.

I turn my attention now to the audio dictation anomalous voice recording. It was not until the day after the investigation, when I played my tapes back, that I heard what I had recorded.

Suzanne and myself were in the office upstairs and we were calling out to the lady who had recently asked, 'Can you help me?' Unbeknown to us at the time another voice was recorded and this time it was that of a man. The disturbing thing about this recording is that he says nothing but my name, 'DARREN!'

To hear such an EVP of what we presume is a ghost or spirit is one thing, but to hear one call your name is something else. Now we know there was only the two of us in the room, and the other group was investigating another part of the building, so the chance of it being one of the other male investigators is impossible. This recording and the other EVPs left us all dumbfounded.

It was now 5 a.m. and time to call it a night. The only thing that remains to be said is that a second investigation at these premises must be held to find out exactly what is going on. With most paranormal investigations and hauntings you are left with more questions than answers, and this case study is no different. Who is the lady that is asking for help? Can the historical records show there was indeed an Irish woman who lived or died there, and who is the spirit that called my name? All these questions are being addressed as we speak and, by the time I come to write another book, we may just have some answers.

Trigger objects placed in a flour tray.

The same trigger objects but this time the battery has been pushed over. (Note – It did not fall but was pressed deeply into the flour.)

Drew Bartley uses his night vision camera in the hope of filming some paranormal activity. This was the room where the voices were recorded.

The Dog and Gun Pub

The Dog and Gun public house is in the Bear Park area of Durham (which is just on the outskirts of the city) and it was at this former coaching inn at Auton Style that our team came to investigate on a cold and snowy winter's night in late 2008. After we had heard that the landlady was having a few minor problems, we contacted the pub owners via a colleague of ours, and sought permission to come in and run some tests.

Fiona Vipond's friend, Yvonne Moore from Sunderland, has a sister and it is Yvonne's sister, Margaret Wilkinson, who owns the Dog and Gun with her husband David Williams. After securing the investigation for Saturday 13 December 2008, we all met up and made our way there. We arrived at the pub at about 10.30 p.m. giving us just enough time to have a few refreshing drinks of still orange before closing time. Of course, the smell of the beers and lagers were tempting us somewhat but being professionals we resisted the temptation.

Snow often lies for longer in Durham than in surrounding areas, as it is considerably higher, and Bear Park is no different. Thick flakes of pure white snow were dropping through the night sky and before long the land was covered with what looked like a soft white untouched blanket. Ice had gripped the road too, making driving conditions rather dangerous to say the least, which was quite worrying as team investigator Mark Winter had yet to arrive.

At 11.15 p.m. Mark did arrive, safe and sound, just in time to help take some general view shots and footage for the investigation DVD. After taking more video footage inside the pub I was ready to interview the pub owner, Margaret. I had decided to wait until the bar was completely empty before attempting to chat with the landlady simply because, prior to that time, she was quite busy. When we were all ready we sat in the bar and commenced with a general chat to see just what had been going on at this pub in the past.

The Dog and Gun public house in Bear Park. A very interesting night was had here by the author.

The first question I asked was how long Margaret and David had been running the pub to which she answered, 'seven years in April.' I then asked her to answer my next question with a simple yes or no. I asked her, 'Is the pub haunted?' She paused for a moment and said, 'Yes… but I have not personally seen anything.' I then asked her why she thought the pub might have been haunted. She went on to say:

There was one occasion. I never actually saw anything but I heard something. I was on my own late at night and was doing the till and all I had on was the light that shines over the till. Suddenly I heard a whispering and it occurred to me that I may have locked some customers in the pub so I put the main lights on and had a look around and found nothing. The whispering, which was garbled and unintelligible, was coming over from the back door entrance at the rear of the pub and it sounded like it was more than one person that was engaged in conversation. It was as though a number of people were having a conversation quietly in the corner there. I even went upstairs to check there and found all quiet. I got my dog and came back down into the bar for a final look around and the voices and whispering had ceased. I took one last look around and then retired to bed thinking nothing more of it.

I then asked Margaret if anyone else had had any odd paranormal experiences at the pub and she went on to say,

'Not when I worked here, but there was a barmaid that worked at the pub and she often saw it! For years she wouldn't go down in the cellar because she always said that it was in there, either there, or in the ladies' loos.'

I then asked her if she could tell us what 'It' really is.

'An old-ish gentleman with an old style long black coat on,' she replied. 'She told me it was an old man, and that's all I wanted to know…I didn't want to know any more to be honest.'

I had heard that another 'spooky' happening had taken place quite recently involving one of Margaret's barmaids so I decided to bring this up to find out just what had happened. She went on to tell me:

Yes, that was one of my barmaids and it happened only a year or two ago. Everyone had left the building and I was standing talking to the barmaid. She too was ready to leave for the night but mentioned that she must pay a visit before heading off. I mentioned to my husband that he might as well just go straight upstairs, and I would finish up in the bar. Just as my barmaid came along the passageway and reached the doorway, she didn't half jump. She told me that she thought Dave had pinched her bottom but after realising he was not there she became frightened. I could tell she was genuine as I saw her jump when something touched her. She said whatever it was really hurt her and for days afterwards she had a bruise on her backside the size of an orange and it was a long, long time before she would come back inside the pub.

I then asked if there was anything else of interest that could be said, to give me a better idea of what may be happening. She went on to say:

At one time, there was a relief bar manager that was put in here on a temporary basis and was supposed to run the pub for a few months. Now I don't know why, but after only one night, she and her husband packed up their belongings and left the pub. Something must have freaked them out so they left, that's all I can surmise. These are the stories you hear…I don't know why they left but I do know they left after only one night.

My penultimate question was whether or not any odd activity, or anything unexplained occurred upstairs in the private living quarters and was told there had not been. I then asked if there was anything else she could think of to make her think the place could be haunted. She thought carefully for a minute and suddenly remembered something:

You know David often gets up in the night and comes down into the bar because he can hear noises and things as if someone is moving around. He does that quite a lot and never actually finds anything…the alarms sometimes trip for no reason too.

So, it seems there is an apparition that haunts the cellars and the ladies' loos, along with a spectral inhabitant that likes to touch people. Could this ghost be one and the same? Or is there more than one spirit residing at the Dog and Gun pub? It all seemed fascinating and we were very much looking forward to beginning the investigation.

Trigger objects were placed in and around the various 'hotspots' in the pub, including a cross that was left down in the cellars. Another cross was drawn around and left at the top of the stairs leading into the cellars and various sets of motion sensors were left in and around the building. A lock off video camera was also left recording down in the cellars in the hope that we could catch the apparition on film. Our pre-investigation baselines showed nothing untoward, with temperatures averaging at normal and all other tests including the EMF sweeps showing no anomalous readings. We were now ready to split into groups and begin the night vigils.

Joining us on tonight's investigation were a few friends of the team. Yvonne, of course, joined us since it was her sister's pub we were investigating, as did usual guest investigators Paul and James Collins, and Andrew Hughes. Drew's eldest son Ryan Bartley was also joining us on his first overnight paranormal investigation. Along with the team members, and Margaret, there were more than enough people to thoroughly investigate the premises.

The vigils began with my group staking out the cellar. Paul Collins and I ventured down there first and began whilst we waited for Margaret and Yvonne to join us. I turned on the video camera and began to film with my night vision video camera. I called out to the atmosphere and asked a few general questions whilst recording them on my EVP machine. I then began to feel dizzy and disorientated, but I put this down to either being a little tired, or perhaps being thrown into the darkness.

Soon, Yvonne and Margaret joined us and the vigil began properly. We all made ourselves comfortable and sat and observed but the only thing worthy of note was that Yvonne and I saw a clear light move across the top of the room near where the wall meets the ceiling. Since there was a tiny aperture in the ceiling, I thought this light might have come from the group that was investigating the pool room area (which was directly above us) but methodical investigating and subsequent tests proved this was not the case. It must be stressed that before we came out of the cellars I made an appeal to any spirits that may have been down there with us. I specifically asked them if they could touch Fiona (sorry Fi) later on when she ventured down there for her vigil. I specified that they perhaps touch her on her neck or her bottom before leaving, and we told no one at all of our little experiment. I thought it would be interesting to see if Fiona reported this later on.

Drew's group proved a little more exciting than ours with some bizarre activity being recorded. Ryan Bartley told me that during their vigil they set up a little experiment with the white pool ball and the pool chalk. During their vigil he told me that 'a shuffling of footsteps' was heard while they were attempting a small séance. No one was moving at the time and the footfalls were on the wooden floor in the very room they were in. 'There was no mistaking it,' he told me. Drew concurred, and said, 'It was really strange.' A knock was heard coming from the picture on the wall behind Jimmy's head and Ryan heard a strange breath. By far the strangest thing that happened was when they found a beer mat on the pool table that was most certainly not there when they set up the pool ball and chalk experiment. 'No one knows how it got there, it's a mystery,' Drew said.

In Fiona's group, while investigating the main bar area, they noticed that the crucifix which had been placed down at the top of the cellar stairs had been slightly moved. They all experienced some quite severe drops in temperature, which in Fiona's words 'simply can't be explained at this point in time.' So, it wasn't a bad start to the investigation and I was hoping that more of the same could be observed.

My group then ventured into the pool room area, while Fiona and co. headed down the cellars, and Drew's group investigated the main bar. It was 2.45 a.m. when the vigil commenced. I set up my video camera recording the pool table in the desperate hope that the 'beer mat' incident would repeat itself. Did it? Of course it didn't, but it was worth a try anyway. At 3.05, while we were discussing something, I heard a noise that sounded like a cough. I asked if anyone was present and no one coughed up to it (pardon the pun). I checked my video camera, as it was recording at the time, and found to my delight the anomalous sound had been picked up on the tape. Nothing else occurred during our vigil; however, at the end of our stint in there at 3.18 a.m. Drew came over and joined us from his vigil.

As we were discussing the vigils, myself, Paul, Drew and Margaret all heard a crystal clear disembodied breath emanating from somewhere within the area. Interestingly, if the reader recalls, Ryan Bartley had also heard a breath just like the one we heard during his first vigil in there earlier on. This breath was also a new paranormal experience for Margaret and it rattled her somewhat as she was expecting very little, or even nothing at all, to happen.

Fiona and Mark had a fascinating vigil too with some scary phenomena occurring. All saw the pulsing phenomenon occurring down there and Mark and Fiona were convinced that the black figure of a man was circling them, for what reasons they don't know.

The beer mat photographed in situ after it was found on the pool table during a vigil in the bar area. It was not there at the beginning of the vigil.

Pulsing, for those who don't know, is when a certain part of the room goes darker than usual and then returns to normal. Was this a trick of the light? Were the investigators' eyes playing tricks on them? Or was it a paranormal phenomenon?

This pulsing creates yet more questions, so more research is needed by paranormal investigators to find out what it actually is. Whatever it is, it's pretty harrowing, as those who have been on paranormal investigations will testify.

Anyway, when Fiona and Mark called out to the atmosphere and asked if there was more than one person with them they all heard a voice simply say 'Three'. It is also very interesting to note that Fiona complained of being touched on the neck and shoulders during her vigil, and when none of the investigators were standing anywhere near her. I must ask the reader to recall that I had specifically asked if any spirits would show Fiona a sign by touching her when she came down here later on. I guess they must have been listening. I must admit Fiona is one of the bravest girls I have met and worked with, with nothing much fazing her in regards to investigating the paranormal.

When she came out of the cellars she was clearly shaken up, so something genuine must have happened down there. When I told her about my little experiment in regards to her being touched she was really shocked, yet ecstatic about the whole thing. I knew Fiona could handle this sort of stuff, which is why I chose her for this experiment. It worked incredibly well, indicating that something was definitely going on. Granted, it was not really scientific and objective, but a personal result for the team nonetheless.

Drew's vigil in the main bar area yielded an interesting result, with Ryan filming a shadow moving from one wall near the kitchen area into the landing area at the top of the stairwell that leads to the cellar. Drew did not know this at the time as Ryan had kept it quiet thinking he must have been mistaken, until Drew mentioned during the vigil that he saw a solid figure of a man moving around on three occasions. Is it a coincidence or not that Fiona's group all heard the word 'three' during their vigil then?

After the break, Drew and Fiona headed off back down in the cellar to further investigate it. Just prior to them going down there we all heard movement coming from within the cellar. With no one down there at that time, we were dumbfounded as to what the noises were. During this stint, it was reported that whatever was down there with them was beginning to get a little aggressive – perhaps because Drew was beginning to aggravate it with a technique known as 'bating'. Bating is a method used to anger the spirit into an outward manifestation and can have devastating results as the author found out many years ago after my privates were squeezed (tightly) by an evil spirit that I was annoying. I literally crawled out of the room in agony and chose not to try this method any more. It is not recommended at all.

Anyway, something large and metallic was hurled across the cellar and hit the cooler fans with considerable force, making quite a loud din. Had the object hit one of the investigators down there it would have resulted in serious injury. This sound, along with the panic and expletives that followed, was recorded on tape. Nothing at all happened on our latest vigil while investigating the bar area. I had locked off my video camera in the direction of the door area where the figure had been seen earlier on with nothing anomalous at all being recorded. I had taken a picture down in the area of the back doors and thought I may have caught an apparition on film, but later inspection of the picture on my computer proved that this was

The area of the pub where a figure was seen by numerous individuals as it moved back and forth in the darkness.

An artist's impression of the 'apparitional male figure' as it stands in the doorway and corridor of the Dog and Gun pub. (Illustration by Julie Olley)

nothing more than an odd reflection from the camera flashlight that was being projected down the back door of the premises.

It was now nearly 5 o'clock and the end of the investigation was nigh. The snow thankfully had ceased falling through the night and we were able to get home. The thought occurred by morning that we might very well be snowed in and unable to leave Durham, which would have been quite frustrating as by this point we were all very tired, but as it happened, we were ok. We all had a good night of investigating with some very odd activity being recorded and documented. It seems there may well be an active spirit residing there at the Dog and Gun, with the activity occurring on our investigation supporting the phenomena that had been reported there prior to our arrival. I will now leave the last word of this chapter to Ryan Bartley, whose investigation there was his very first:

In all honesty I expected nothing to happen and that would just be my luck. My dad [Drew] tells me all about the investigations you guys do and they sound great. As it happens I did have a good investigation and I experienced my first paranormal activity including the breaths, other odd sounds that can't be accounted for, and most strangely the beer mat incident. Yes, it was a good night and I am so glad to be able to say that I was a part of it.

AFTERWORD

Writing, researching and preparing *Haunted Durham* was, for me, a total joy. After completing *Haunted Newcastle* I needed another similar project to sink my teeth into, so when the opportunity arose for the *Haunted Durham* book, I grabbed it with both hands. Durham City is only 18 miles from Newcastle so it was not a problem getting there to do my work. I had visited Durham City on dozens of occasions for various reasons and always found the place to be a place of charm.

I thought I knew Durham City quite well until I began my research for this book. I quickly found out that there was much more to this historical city than meets the eye – many more places of interest and many more areas of importance and significance. I discovered many wonderful nooks and crannies that the everyday visitor to Durham might easily miss. During my visits there I must have paced the streets back and forth, up and down and from one end of the city to the other in my pursuit of its fêted ghosts and in hope of finding some new ones. I didn't realise that researching books could be so physically demanding! After my days in Durham my limbs ached from the tips of my toes to the tops of my thighs with all the walking I did, but I have to say it was worth every second – what a delight.

Durham City hasn't that many ghost legends to tell so I can't see it being labelled 'the most haunted city', but like most places, it has its fair share of resident phantoms and poltergeists. Part of the enjoyment in researching books like this is digging out and finding brand new accounts that no one has ever heard before. Naturally, re-telling the good, classic ghost tales is just as essential, because keeping these legends alive for future generations to hear and learn about is fundamental to our heritage. Provided that the tales being re-told are as close to the real truth as they were when they were first told, there is nothing wrong in keeping the tradition of ghost lore alive.

Bringing together this astonishing assemblage of ghost narratives that are associated with Durham, a beautiful and remarkable city, really has been labour of love. After visiting the many locations that are featured within these pages, and listening to so many people from all walks of life as they speak of their strange, yet fascinating, accounts of a world that lies just beyond our own senses, makes me realise that there must be something else going on in our world that we

Durham Cathedral and Castle viewed from Crook Hall.

don't yet understand. It also makes my job as an investigator and writer a whole lot easier and more pleasurable.

Supping the occasional pint of ale, and listening to landlords and patrons regale us with stories of ghosts and spectres, is not work. The same applies to being shown around extraordinary and historic properties by their respective guardians or curator – also a very pleasant and

enlightening experience. As I learn the histories and soak up the ambience of wherever I may be, I attempt to reach far back in time and metaphorically touch what was once there many years ago and at the same time hoping, just hoping, that the resident ghost decides to make its appearance during my visit.

When I look back at what has been achieved, I take great delight in the fact that now, a lot of my work is in print, and folk from all over the North of England – and beyond – may very well own copies of my books and read up on my spooky adventures. If I have raised an eyebrow, made someone stop and think, or maybe even given someone the encouragement to get up and do some of their own ghost research, I will know it has all been worthwhile.

I suppose when I reflect on what I do I question myself and contemplate why this line of work is 'a labour of love'. It's a funny phrase isn't it? I mean…who enjoys work? Love, it most certainly is. The labour – if you can call it that – actually begins back at home when I start to write up my adventures. Having said that, sitting at my PC mulling over the events, with my fingers giving it 'fifty to the dozen' is almost as enjoyable as the actual field research itself. Going through my written notes and listening to my pre-recorded conversations, trying not to miss any of the detail while documenting my findings is quite therapeutic and extremely satisfying. This type of work I can deal with.

Anyway, that said…I really hope that you, the reader, have taken great pleasure in meandering through these pages, being enthralled by the many fabulous ghost tales and strange accounts that the City of Durham has to offer. I hope you have enjoyed reading about them as much as I have enjoyed investigating them and writing them up.

BIBLIOGRAPHY & RECOMMENDED READING

BOOKS

Day, James Wentworth, *In Search of Ghosts* (Muller, 1969)

Dodds, Derek, *Northumbria at War* (Pen and Sword, 2005)

Haining, Peter, *Ghosts*, (BCA, 1974)

Hallowell, Michael J. & Ritson, Darren W., *Ghost Taverns* (Amberley, 2009)

Hallowell, Michael J., *Christmas Ghost Stories* (Amberley, 2008)

Hallum, Jack, *Ghosts of the North* (David & Charles, 1976)

Hapgood, Sarah, *500 British Ghosts and Hauntings* (Foulsham, 1993)

Harper, Charles G., *Haunted Houses* (Senate, 1907)

Harries, John, *The Ghost Hunter's Road Book* (Letts, 1968)

Hippisley Coxe, Antony D., *Haunted Britain* (Pan, 1973)

Hugill, Robert, *Castles of Durham* (Frank Graham 1979)

Lyndon Dodds, Glen, *Historic Sites of Northumberland and Newcastle-upon-Tyne* (Albion Press, 2002)

MacKenzie, Andrew, *Hauntings and Apparitions* (Heinemann, 1982)

Maple, Eric, *Supernatural England* (Hale, 1977)

O'Donnell, Elliot, *Haunted Britain* (Rider, 1948)

Poole, Keith B., *Haunted Heritage* (Guild Publishing, 1988)

Price, Harry, *Poltergeist over England* (Country Life Ltd, 1945)

Puttick, Betty, *Supernatural England* (Countryside Books, 2002)

Ritson, Darren W., *Haunted Newcastle* (The History Press, 2009)

Ritson, Darren W., *Ghost Hunter: True Life Encounters from the North East* (GHP, 2006)

Ritson, Darren W., *In Search of Ghosts: Real Hauntings From Around Britain* (Amberley, 2008)

Underwood, Peter, *This Haunted Isle* (Harrap, 1984)

Underwood, Peter, *Gazetteer of British Ghosts* (Souvenir Press, 1971)

Underwood, Peter, *The A-Z of British Ghosts* (Souvenir Press, 1971)

WEBSITES

Capital punishment UK – http://www.capitalpunishmentuk.org/contents.html

The paranormal database – http://www.paranormaldatabase.com/

David Simpson – http://www.northeastengland.talktalk.net/DavidSimpsonHistory.html

API – http://www.anomalous-phenomena-investigations.co.uk

Other titles published by The History Press

Haunted Newcastle

DARREN W. RITSON

This fascinating book contains over forty-five spine-chilling accounts from in and around central Newcastle. Discover poltergeists, apparitions, curses, hauntings and even the ghost of a living person! From the ancient city walls to the cobbled back streets of old Newcastle, and including graveyards, museums, stately halls, pubs, parks and monasteries, this book includes many pulse-raising narratives that are guaranteed to make your blood run cold.

978 0 7524 4880 0

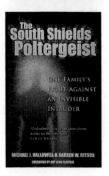

The South Shields Poltergeist

MICHAEL J. HALLOWELL AND DARREN W. RITSON

In December 2005 a family began to experience poltergeist-like phenomena in their home. Slowly but steadily the phenomena escalated, and in July 2006 the authors were asked to investigate. This book details their investigation into what they believe to be the most protracted and documented case of its kind.

978 0 7524 5274 6

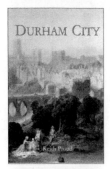

Durham City

K. PROUD

The City of Durham was founded in AD 995. The author bases his definitive study on scholarly research, and tells Durham's remarkable story in the language of a skilled communicator. It is a tale of saints and sinners, of bishops and battles, deans and demagogues, of monarchs and men, set against and within one of the most magnificent architectural backdrops in the world.

978 1 8607 7249 8

Durham Railways

CHARLIE EMETT

This fascinating selection of over 250 photographs takes the reader on a journey from the pioneering beginnings, through the revolutionary age of steam and the diesel era, to today's electric expresses, drawn by the most powerful locomotives ever to run in Britain. Famous engines, signalling systems, personalities and events of the region are all recorded here, offering the reader a comprehensive picture of railway life over the years.

978 0 7524 4955 5

Visit our website and discover thousands of other History Press books.

www.thehistorypress.co.uk

Printed in Great Britain
by Amazon